FTCE Guidance and Counseling PK-12
Teacher Certification Exam

By: Sharon Wynne, M.S.

XAMonline, INC.
Boston

Copyright © 2008 XAMonline, Inc.
All rights reserved. No part of the material protected by this copyright notice may be reproduced or utilized in any form or by any means, electronic or mechanical, including photocopying, recording or by any information storage and retrievable system, without written permission from the copyright holder.

To obtain permission(s) to use the material from this work for any purpose including workshops or seminars, please submit a written request to:

XAMonline, Inc.
25 First Street, Suite 106
Cambridge, MA 02141
Toll Free 1-800-509-4128
Email: info@xamonline.com
Web www.xamonline.com
Fax: 1-617-583-5552

Library of Congress Cataloging-in-Publication Data

Guidance and Counseling PK-12: Teacher Certification / Sharon A. Wynne. -2nd ed.
ISBN 978-1-58197-586-4
1. Guidance and Counseling PK-12.   2. Study Guides.   3. FTCE
4. Teachers' Certification & Licensure.   5. Careers

Disclaimer:
The opinions expressed in this publication are the sole works of XAMonline and were created independently from the National Education Association, Educational Testing Service, or any State Department of Education, National Evaluation Systems or other testing affiliates.

Between the time of publication and printing, state specific standards as well as testing formats and website information may change that is not included in part or in whole within this product. Sample test questions are developed by XAMonline and reflect similar content as on real tests; however, they are not former tests. XAMonline assembles content that aligns with state standards but makes no claims nor guarantees teacher candidates a passing score. Numerical scores are determined by testing companies such as NES or ETS and then are compared with individual state standards. A passing score varies from state to state.

Printed in the United States of America   œ-1

FTCE: Guidance and Counseling PK-12
ISBN: 978-1-58197-586-4

TEACHER CERTIFICATION STUDY GUIDE

XAMonline.com
Teacher Certification Specialists

Your state. . . Your test. . .Your XAM

It's natural to be nervous about taking your state teacher certification exam. Rest assured that **XAM** test preparation guides contain everything you need to excel.

XAM offers the most comprehensive line of teacher certification exam preparation books available on the market. We're committed to providing aspiring public school professionals with the very best test preparation guides because we believe that higher quality study guides lead to higher quality teachers.

State-specific certification test study guides are extremely hard to find, and **XAM** is the only test preparation company offering complete depth and breadth of subjects and states, across the country. All of our exam preparation materials include all required competencies and skills overviews, as well as a full complement of sample test questions that mirror the actual certification tests.

You won't find another company with a wider range of certification test preparation books, anywhere. We are the state certification exam test preparation experts.

Thorough certification test preparation is utterly *essential* to your future as a public school professional, and **XAM** study guides will enable you to approach your examination with confidence, knowing you are thoroughly and comprehensively prepared.

Get Certified. Get XAM.

SCHOOL COUNSELING

: TEACHER CERTIFICATION STUDY GUIDE

Table of Contents

COMPETENCY 1.0   KNOWLEDGE OF COUNSELING 1

Skill 1.1   Basic Concepts of Major Counseling Theories 1

Skill 1.2   Counseling Theories in Relation to Personality, Learning and Human Development Theory 35

Skill 1.3   Application of Counseling Theories and Techniques to a Specific Situation 40

Skill 1.4   Merits and Limitations of Individual and Group Counseling 42

Skill 1.5   Group Dynamics 44

Skill 1.6   Communication Skills 46

Skill 1.7   Stressors Affecting Students and School Performance 49

Skill 1.8   Guidance Activities 59

Skill 1.9   Communicating Information to Students 63

Skill 1.10   Resources and Evaluation Materials for Counseling Activities 65

COMPETENCY 2.0   KNOWLEDGE OF STUDENT APPRAISAL 70

Skill 2.1   Knowledge of Measurement Concepts 70

Skill 2.2   Conditions Affecting Test Results 71

Skill 2.3   Major Functions of Appraisal 72

Skill 2.4   Procedures Involved in Appraisal Administration 74

Skill 2.5   Reporting Assessment Results to Students and Parents 75

Skill 2.6   Understanding the Statistics Essential for Interpretation 78

Skill 2.7   Sharing Data with Other Professionals both inside and Outside the School 79

Skill 2.8   Interpret Student Data From Written Reports 79

TEACHER CERTIFICATION STUDY GUIDE

COMPETENCY 3.0 KNOWLEDGE OF EDUCATION AND CAREER DEVELOPMENT 81

Skill 3.1 Knowledge of Similarities and Differences of Career Development Theories 81

Skill 3.2 Career Development Activities 85

Skill 3.3 Relating Decision-making Processes to Career Development 87

Skill 3.4 Evaluation of Educational and Career Materials............................... 89

Skill 3.5 Identification of Appropriate Materials for Educational and Career Development 91

Skill 3.6 Interpret Student Appraisal Data Relevant to Career Development 92

Skill 3.7 Assist Students in Developing Employability Skills and Exploring Education and Training Options 94

COMPETENCY 4.0 KNOWLEDGE OF CONSULTATION 98

Skill 4.1 Components of a Consultation Prototype 98

Skill 4.2 Procedures for Problem Solving 101

Skill 4.3 Communication the Needs of Students 102

Skill 4.4 Communicating with Parents 102

Skill 4.5 Efficient Use of Data and Resources 103

Skill 4.6 Identifying Transition and Follow-Up Procedures 103

TEACHER CERTIFICATION STUDY GUIDE

COMPETENCY 5.0 KNOWLEDGE OF COORDINATION 105

Skill 5.1 Collect and Synthesize Student Referral Data 105

Skill 5.2 Referral Procedures for In-School and Out-of-School Individuals and Agencies 105

Skill 5.3 Informing the Community of Guidance Services 106

Skill 5.4 Organizing and Administering the Guidance Program 107

Skill 5.5 Creating an Orientation Meeting for Students to the School and Guidance Program 109

COMPETENCY 6.0 KNOWLEDGE OF PROFESSIONAL, ETHICAL AND LEGAL CONSIDERATIONS 111

Skill 6.1 Legal Mandates and Ethical Standards Regarding Assessment Data 111

Skill 6.2 Professional Standards of the American School Counseling Association and American Counseling Association 111

Skill 6.3 Legal Rights of Students and Parents Concerning Student Records 114

Skill 6.4 Legislation and Special Needs Students 115

Skill 6.5 Laws Regarding Child Abuse and Neglect 118

COMPETENCY 7.0 KNOWLEDGE OF PLACEMENT 121

Skill 7.1 Learning Styles and Individual Differences 121

Skill 7.2 Post Secondary Educational Opportunities 124

Skill 7.3 Locating and Securing Financial Aid Assistance and Scholarships 125

COMPETENCY 8.0	KNOWLEDGE OF RESEARCH, EVALUATION AND FOLLOW-UP	127
Skill 8.1	Steps in Research, Evaluation, and Follow-Up	127
Skill 8.2	Needs Assessment and Program Evaluation Techniques	130
Skill 8.3	Interpretation of the Results of Research, Evaluation, and Follow-Up	132
Skill 8.4	Developing Program Objectives and Determining Appropriate Outcomes Based on Assessment Data	132
COMPETENCY 9.0	KNOWLEDGE OF CURRENT TRENDS AND TECHNIQUES	135
Skill 9.1	Prevention and Positive School Environments	135
Skill 9.2	Crisis Management	137
Skill 9.3	Using Technology Effectively	139

Bibliography 141

Sample Test 144

Answer Key 174

Rigor Table 174

Rationales for Sample Questions 176

TEACHER CERTIFICATION STUDY GUIDE

Great Study and Testing Tips!

What to study in order to prepare for the subject assessments is the focus of this study guide but equally important is *how* you study.

You can increase your chances of truly mastering the information by taking some simple yet effective steps.

Study Tips:

1. Some foods aid the learning process.

Foods such as milk, nuts, seeds, rice, and oats help your study efforts by releasing natural memory enhancers called CCKs (*cholecystokinin*) composed of *tryptopha*n, *choline* and *phenylalanine*. All of these chemicals enhance the neurotransmitters associated with memory.

Before studying, try a light, protein-rich meal of eggs, turkey or fish. All of these foods release memory-enhancing chemicals. The better the connections in your brain, the more you comprehend. Likewise, before you take a test, stick to a light snack of energy-boosting and relaxing foods. A glass of milk, a piece of fruit, or some peanuts all contain CCKs and help you to relax and focus on the subject at hand.

2. Learn to take great notes.

We learn best when information is organized. When it has a logical structure and we can see relationships between pieces of information helps us assimilate new information.

If your notes are scrawled all over the paper, it fragments the flow of the information. Instead, strive for clarity. Newspapers, for example, use a standard format to achieve clarity. Your notes can be much clearer through use of proper formatting. A very effective format is called the *"Cornell Method."*

> Take a sheet of loose-leaf lined notebook paper and draw a line all the way down the paper about 1-2" from the left-hand edge.
>
> Draw another line across the width of the paper about 1-2" up from the bottom. Repeat this process on the reverse side of the page.

Look at the highly effective result. You have ample room for notes, a left hand margin for special emphasis items or inserting supplementary data from the textbook, a large area at the bottom for a brief summary, and a little rectangular space for just about anything you want.

3. Get the concept and then the details.

Too often we focus on the details and don't grasp an understanding of the concept. However, if you simply memorize only dates, places, or names, you may well miss the whole point of the subject.

A key way to understand things is to put them in your own words. If you are working from a textbook, automatically summarize each paragraph in your mind. If you are outlining text, don't simply copy the author's words.

Rephrase them in your own words. You remember your own thoughts and words much better than someone else's, and will subconsciously tend to associate the important details to the core concepts.

4. Ask why.

Pull apart written material paragraph by paragraph – and don't forget the captions under the illustrations.

If you train your mind to think in a series of questions and answers, not only will you learn more, but you will also have less test anxiety because you are used to answering questions.

Example: If the heading is "Stream Erosion", flip it around to read "Why do streams erode?" Then answer the questions.

5. Read for reinforcement and future needs.

Even if you only have 10 minutes, put your notes or a book in your hand. Your mind is similar to a computer; you have to input data in order to have it processed. *By reading, you are creating the neural connections for future retrieval.* The more times you read something, the more you reinforce the learning of ideas.

Even if you don't fully understand something on the first pass, *your mind stores much of the material for later recall.*

6. Relax to learn: in other words, go into exile.

Our bodies respond to an inner clock called biorhythms. Burning the midnight oil works well for some people, but not others.

If possible, set aside a particular place to study that is free of distractions. Shut off the television, cell phone and pager, and exile your friends and family during your study period.

If you really are bothered by silence, try background music. Light classical music at a low volume has been shown to aid in concentration over other types of music. Music that evokes pleasant emotions without lyrics is highly suggested. Try just about anything by Mozart. It can relax you.

7. Use arrows not highlighters.

At best, it's difficult to read a page full of yellow, pink, blue, and green streaks. Try staring at a neon sign for a while and you'll soon see that the horde of colors obscures the message.

A quick note, a brief dash of color, an underline or an arrow pointing to a particular passage is much clearer than a cascade of highlighted words.

8. Budget your study time.

Although you shouldn't ignore any of the material, *allocate your available study time in the same ratio that topics may appear on the test.* In other words, focus on the areas that are most likely to be included in the test.

Testing Tips:

1. Get smart by playing dumb. Don't read anything into the question.

Don't make an assumption that the test writer is looking for something other than what is asked. Stick to the question as written and don't read anything into it.

2. Read the question and all the choices *twice* before answering the question.

You may miss something by not carefully reading, and then re-reading both the question and the answers.

If you really don't have a clue as to the right answer, leave it blank on the first time through. Go on to the other questions, as they may provide a clue as to how to answer the skipped questions.

If later on, you still can't answer the skipped ones . . . *Guess.* The only penalty for guessing is that you *might* get it wrong. One thing is certain; if you don't put anything down, you will get it wrong!

TEACHER CERTIFICATION STUDY GUIDE

3. Turn the question into a statement.

Look at the way the questions are worded. The syntax of the question usually provides a clue. Does it seem more familiar as a statement rather than as a question? Does it sound strange?

By turning a question into a statement, you may be able to spot if an answer sounds right, and it may also trigger memories of material you have read.

4. Look for hidden clues.

It's actually very difficult to compose multiple-foil (choice) questions without giving away part of the answer in the options presented.

In most multiple-choice questions, you can often readily eliminate one or two of the potential answers. This leaves you with only two real possibilities and automatically your odds go to fifty-fifty with very little work.

5. Trust your instincts.

For every fact you have read, you subconsciously retain something of that knowledge. On questions that you aren't really certain about, go with your basic instincts. **Your first impression on how to answer a question is usually correct.**

6. Mark your answers directly on the test booklet.

Don't bother trying to fill in the optical scan sheet on the first pass through the test. *Just be very careful not to miss-mark your answers when you eventually transcribe them to the scan sheet.*

7. Watch the clock!

You have a set amount of time to answer the questions. Don't get bogged down trying to answer a single question at the expense of 10 questions you can answer more readily.

TEACHER CERTIFICATION STUDY GUIDE

The Florida Teacher Certification Exam (FTCE)
Guidance and Counseling PK-12

The Florida Teacher Certification Exam is generally 2 and 1/2 hours in length. You will be tested on a wide variety of information, which is based on the expected competencies as found in this test booklet. It is difficult to predict exactly what is going to be on each exam, which is why it is very important to thoroughly review information pertaining to all of the required competencies.

Test results on the FTCE are reported as pass/fail scores. This means that there is a minimal level of knowledge that you are expected to possess in order to obtain licensure. The expectations are in line with what you have studied in your academic coursework, but a thorough review is necessary before taking such an important test. You can get an overview of what you will be tested on by reading over the headings in the Table of Contents.

Each competency (and sub-competency) is then explained in detail for you, followed by a summary at the end of each of the nine major competency sections. We suggest beginning with the areas in which you feel you need the most help and then reading over the other areas. Do not feel as though you need to read through the competencies in order. The night before the exam, review the summary boxes.

TEACHER CERTIFICATION STUDY GUIDE

COMPETENCY 1.0   KNOWLEDGE OF COUNSELING

SKILL 1.1   Basic Concepts of Major Counseling Theories

There are many theories in the literature of human and personality development as well as in counseling and psychotherapy. The major theories explored in this section are psychoanalytic theory (as created by Freud and developed by his followers) the psychodynamic models of Erikson and Adler, behaviorism, cognitive-behavior therapy, existentialism, person-centered therapy, Gestalt therapy, reality therapy, and solution-focused therapy.

PSYCHOANALYTIC THEORY

The basis of most theories of psychology and counseling evolves from the psychoanalytic theory of **Sigmund Freud**. Other theorists who embraced psychoanalytic theory were Otto Rank, Heinz Hartman, Ernest Jones, Anna Freud, Alfred Adler, Heinz Kohut, Erik Erikson, Carl Jung, Karen Horney, Harry Stack Sullivan, John Bowlby, Margaret Mahler, Jacques Lacan, and Nancy Chodorow. Many broadened Freud's original ideas into different schools; these are often collectively referred to as psychodynamic theory and therapy.

Freud viewed human behavior as primarily the manifestation of biological and instinctive drives, unconscious motivation, and irrational forces. He divided the personality into the following parts:

- the ID, the part of the personality that is blind, demanding, pleasure-seeking and insistent; its function is to lessen tension and to return the psyche to a sense of homoeostasis or status quo;
- the EGO, the part of the personality that is the arbitrator between external reality and internal impulses and experiences; and
- the SUPER EGO, the part of the personality representing moral training whose goal is perfection and "doing the right thing".

He also explored the concept of the unconscious by using techniques of dream analysis, post-hypnotic suggestion, and free association. Anxiety and various ego-defense mechanisms were other components of the personality.

Psychoanalytic therapy aims to reconstruct the personality instead of solving immediate problems, with a focus on the past in order to analyze aspects of the unconscious that are manifested in present behavior. Goals for clients include greater insight into their unconscious psychodynamics, an increased ability to understand the connection between their past and present behaviors, and more psychological awareness.

According to psychoanalytic theory, there are five stages of psychosexual development. These stages are:

1. **Oral** - The mouth is the source of satisfaction - If these oral needs are not met, greediness and acquisitiveness may develop as well as the rejection of others' love, fear of intimate relationships, and mistrust of others.

2. **Anal** - Control of the feces is the source of satisfaction - Negative feelings, including rage, hatred, destructiveness and hostility, are experienced if the need to control one's own bodily functions is not successfully resolved.

3. **Phallic** - The phallus (penis/clitoris) are the source of satisfaction - Penis envy and castration anxiety are associated with this stage of development. Resolution of sexual conflicts and sex-role identity is a critical task at this stage with the Electra and Oedipus complexes resulting from difficulties associated with this stage.

4. **Latency** – This stage has been thought to be a relatively calm period of inward and self-centered preoccupation. If not resolved adequately, narcissistic orientation can occur. The latency period usually occurs between the ages of 5 and 12.

5. **Genital** - This stage is signaled by physical maturity. Preoccupation with the sex organs is possible if not adequately resolved.

Psychopathology results from failing to meet one or more critical developmental tasks or becoming fixated at an early level of development. Neurotic personality development is regarded as an incomplete resolution of one of the stages of psychosexual development. Behavior is determined by unconscious forces, early experiences, and sexual and aggressive impetus.

Projection of the client's feelings upon the therapist is used to facilitate therapy; this is called *transference*. TO enhance this process, the therapist tries to remain a "blank slate."

Other techniques used in this therapy include:

1. **Maintaining the Analytic Framework** – The therapist strives to adhere to strict relational rules, including nondisclosure on the part of the therapist/analyst, utilizing psychoanalytic techniques maintaining the contractual agreement for payment of fees, and having sessions regularly and consistently.

2. **Free Association** -This technique encourages the client to say whatever comes to mind in order to reveal the unconscious and give the therapist the opportunity to interpret the unconscious thoughts.

3. **Interpretation** – This is the process of analyzing the material the client reveals from the unconscious via free association and dreams.

4. **Dream Analysis** – This process encourages clients to report and discuss their dreams. The client is then encouraged by the therapist to free associate to various parts of and symbols contained in the dream. The analyst offers interpretations.

5. **Analysis and Interpretation of Resistance** – This technique involves an analysis of the ways the client is resisting the process of change.

6. **Analysis and Interpretation of Transference** – In this approach, the therapist interprets and discusses the significance of the transference process and the therapist-client relationship.

Subsequent developments in psychoanalytic theory that are considered "psychodynamic" are still grounded in key concepts from psychoanalytic theory. These include the role of the unconscious in conscious functioning, the relationship between childhood experiences and adult behavior, a developmental framework of personality, and some of the elements of the therapy process.

However, many of these offshoots are more likely to incorporate ideas about the role of external factors such as other people, the environment, and social norms in the development of personality as well as intervention. These theorists focus upon the ego and its development, as well as the development of the self as an individual.

The goal of these theories is to help the client become more aware of the unconscious, as well as to strengthen the ego system so behavior is based upon reality. Psychodynamic theories include **ego psychology**, **object relations**, **attachment theory**, **psychosocial theory**, **analytical psychology**, and **interpersonal therapy.**

Margaret Mahler was instrumental in developing the object relations theory of psychoanalysis. This theory focuses upon predetermined stages of development in which the child focuses less and less upon self and begins to see the world in relation to others. As development progresses, the child transitions from:

1. "**normal infantile autism**" - where the infant responds to physical stress, does not see a unified self, and considers self and mother as one; to a

2. "**symbiotic relationship**" - with the mother from 1-2 months of age, where the infant is dependent upon the mother and expects emotional congruence with the mother (mother also benefits from the relationship); to a

3. **"separation from this symbiotic relationship"** which occurs as the child gains cognitive awareness of being a separate person around 16-18 months of age; to becoming

4. **"individualized"**, a process that takes place from age 18 months to approximately 3 years of age, and finally; into the

5. **"integration of self"** or maturation as a 3-1/2 – 4 year old.

If a trauma occurs during the separation-individuation phase, borderline and narcissistic personalities often develop; in other words, people often have difficulty with regulating their sense of self and their relationships with others.

More recently, **interpersonal therapy** has emerged from psychoanalytic theories. This time-limited approach also incorporates concepts and structure from cognitive-behavioral therapy and other intervention approaches. It is commonly used with people experiencing depression.

A structural overview of the various concepts and schools of thought in psychoanalytic and psychodynamic theory can be found at en.wikipedia.org/wiki/Psychoanalysis.

Contributions of *psychoanalytic* theory are:
1. This theory is the basis for all psychological theorizing involved in the explanation of human behavior, because it was the first theory.

2. The approach provides a framework for exploring an individual's history and their relationship to the present by way of the unconscious

3. The concept of resolving resistance to the change process is a key aspect of the success of the therapeutic process.

4. Many of the techniques of the therapy can be applied to other therapeutic Models, including the development of interpersonal therapy.

Limitations of *psychoanalytic* and *psychodynamic* theory include:
1. For people utilizing traditional psychoanalytic therapy, a prolonged therapist training period is required. Further, work with clients also tends to be long-term.

2. The importance of action to alleviate the problem is not recognized.

3. The basic concepts of the theory are not verifiable by empirical research.

4. The theory is based on neurotic rather than healthy personalities.

5. The theory cannot be used in crisis counseling where immediate solutions are needed.

6. Traditional psychoanalytic theory does not take into account social, cultural, and interpersonal variables, although some of the derivative schools of thought in psychodynamic theory do.

Some of the key vocabulary terms used in *psychoanalytic* and *psychodynamic* therapy are:

Abreaction - the emotional reliving of past painful experiences.

Anxiety - the result of repressing threatening thoughts or feelings.

Borderline Personality Disorder - the pathology that develops when an individual fails to adequately develop in the separation-individuation phase, characterized by instability, irritability, self-destruction, impulsive anger, and extreme mood shifts.

Compensation - an ego defense mechanism that helps develop positive traits to make up for individual limitations.

Countertransference - a reaction towards the client by the therapist that can interfere with objectivity. It is generally related to the unmet and sometimes unconscious needs of the therapist.

Denial - the distortion of reality in an attempt to avoid dealing with a particular situation.

Displacement - the tendency to point ones' energy toward another person or object in order to reduce ones' own anxiety.

Ego - the part of the personality that mediates between the unconscious instincts and the environment.

Ego-Defense Mechanism - the unconscious process that operate to protect the individual from threatening and anxiety producing thoughts, feelings, and impulses. Examples include displacement, denial, repression and rationalization.

Ego Psychology – a theory of ego development reflecting different stages of life; formulated by Heinz Hartmann, Erik Erikson and other theorists.

Electra Complex - the unconscious sexual feelings of a daughter toward her father coupled with hostility toward her mother.

Free Association - the technique of permitting the client to say whatever comes to mind without censor.

Fixation - the process of getting stuck at a particular stage of psychosexual development.

Id - the part of the personality that is ruled by the pleasure principle. It is the center of the instincts, which are largely unconscious.

Interpretation - a technique of the therapist to explain a particular event or behavior.

Interjection - an ego defense mechanism where the client takes on behavior learned from another.

Libido - the energy of all life instincts including sexual energy.

Narcissistic Personality Disorder - a personality disorder characterized by extreme self-love, an exaggerated sense of self-importance, and an explosive attitude towards others; these attitudes usually hide a poor self-concept.

Object Relations – the theory that describes the interactional system of self and other; this theory is strongly based in developmental concepts.

Oedipus Complex - the unconscious sexual feelings of a son toward his mother coupled with hostility towards his father.

Projection - the tendency on the part of the client to attribute to others the qualities that are unacceptable in his/her own personality.

Psychic Energy - the drive that propels a person's behavior and psychological functioning.

Rationalization - the method of explaining failures or negative occurrences.

Reaction Formation - an ego defense mechanism where a client strives to hide a socially unacceptable thought or feeling with behavior that is considered appropriate.

Regression - an ego defense mechanism of reverting to a less mature stage of development.

Repression - the unconscious act of pushing unacceptable or painful experiences into the unconscious.

Resistance - the client's unwillingness to share feelings and thoughts, or to make changes, in order for the psychoanalytic process to be successful.

Sublimation - the process of redirecting sexual and other biological energies into socially acceptable and creative avenues.

Super Ego - the part of the personality that determines what is right and wrong and strives to "be good."

Symbiosis - a relationship between two individuals that is advantageous or necessary to both. If an individual does not progress beyond this stage, borderline personality disorder can develop.

Transference - the fostering of emotions originally experienced towards one individual upon another individual not connected with the original experience (usually the therapist).

Working Through - the process of exploring unconscious material, ego defenses, transference, and resistance.

ERIKSON'S PSYCHOSOCIAL THEORY OF HUMAN DEVELOPMENT

Erik Erikson built on Freud's work and developed what is referred to as psychosocial theory. It focuses on developmental tasks in relation to self and others. The eight stages of life articulated in this theory are:

1. **Basic Trust vs. Basic Mistrust** – (Birth to approximately 18 months of age). The infant's needs for nourishment and care are satisfied. The response to these needs must be consistent so the infant develops a sense of trust and attachment to one or two adults. Mistrust results if the infant's needs are not met.

2. **Autonomy vs. Shame and Doubt** – (18 to 30 months of age). The child develops an early sense of independence and a measure of some control over the environment. This independence is manifested by self-feeding, dressing, toileting, etc. In this stage the child needs reassurance and support from the adults around him or her Overprotection should be avoided.

3. **Initiative vs. Guilt** – (2-1/2 to 5 years of age). The child develops an imagination and enjoys play-acting adult roles. The child is also learning to perform adult roles and begins to realize restraints are necessary. A pervasive sense of guilt occurs if the child is not successful in initiating everyday activities and tasks.

4. **Industry vs. Inferiority** – (Elementary and middle school years). The child becomes curious with the need to explore and manipulate the environment around her or him. Competency is reached through accomplishments. The child becomes increasingly aware of interactions with others in the school and neighborhood. If a sense of adequacy is not acquired during this stage, feelings of inferiority occur.

5. **Identity vs. Role Confusion** – (Adolescence). The child is striving for an identity and sense of self-worth. Adolescents seek to formulate their own values, beliefs and style of life. They experiment with different lifestyles. If previous stages have not been resolved satisfactorily, the tasks may reoccur here as developmental problems. Resolving unfinished business is one of the major tasks of adolescence.

6. **Intimacy vs. Isolation** - This struggle occurs during young adulthood. The adult becomes willing to be open about self and to commit to a close personal relationship.

7. **Generativity vs. Stagnation** - Maturity is achieved. The task here is to establish and guide the next generation and come to terms with one's dreams and accomplishments.

8. **Ego-Integrity vs. Despair** - This stage occurs during later life. Despair may be experienced by the elderly if ego-integrity is not obtained. When successful, people have a sense of fulfillment about their lives.

ADLERIAN THEORY AND THERAPY

Alfred Adler was originally a follower of Freud. Subsequent Adlerians include **Rudolf Dreikers** and **Harold Mosak**. Rudolf Dreikers was instrumental in applying Adlerian principles to group work. Where Freud explored the psychosexual aspects of personality, Adler concentrated upon the psychosocial aspects of human nature. He believed that people are in control of their lives, thus creating an individual lifestyle at an early age.

Adler called his approach *individual psychology*. In contrast to Freud, Adler felt that consciousness rather than unconsciousness was the core of personality theory. He did not believe in reliving childhood experiences, but instead using these early recollections as clues to understanding the lifestyle of the individual.

Adler emphasized the positive abilities of the individual as influenced by societal forces and the capacity of each to reach optimal development. His theory became the basis for the ensuing humanistic theories that abound today. The main goal is confronting basic mistakes and assumptions the client has made and attempting to redirect them. The focus is on examining the beliefs of the client as expressed by his/her behavior.

Some key concepts in Adler's theory are:

- Childhood experiences are not as crucial in themselves as is the attitude toward these experiences.
- All people have a lifestyle, none of which are the same.
- That lifestyle is set by age 5 and is a reaction to perceived inferiority.
- That lifestyle is learned from early family interactions.
- Behavior is motivated by social needs and has a goal oriented direction.

Therefore, Adlerians are concerned with helping clients change their "basic mistakes" by aiding them in developing positive attitudes and in learning to correct these mistakes.

Four phases of the therapeutic process in Adlerian therapy are:

1. **Establishment of a Therapeutic Relationship** – The therapist joins with the client in a working relationship that is characterized by cooperation, respect and equality, with an emphasis upon joint responsibility.

2. **Analysis and Assessment** - A formal questionnaire is completed in order to ascertain the lifestyle of the individual, to determine early family interactions of each family member, and to obtain as accurate a picture as possible of the client's early social world.

3. **Insight** - The development of the ability to understand past actions with the goal of creating a plan of action for the present.

4. **Reorientation** - This phase involves having the client put insights into positive action with the therapist assisting the client to see new alternatives.

One of the main tools the Adlerian therapist uses is the **Lifestyle Assessment**. This extensive questionnaire about the client's family, childhood memories, dreams, and self-concepts explores birth order, interactions between siblings and parents, and the child's psychological position in the family. The therapist summarizes and interprets these data, and works to make clients more aware of their assumptions about their lifestyle, their "basic mistakes," and the self-defeating attitudes they still utilize.

The birth order of a child can indicate certain types of behavior. The oldest child usually receives a great deal of attention, is dependable and hardworking, and strives to keep ahead. The second child attempts to compete with the older sibling. The middle child tends to feel left out and develops an attitude that life is unfair. The youngest child tends to be the most pampered, plays a special role and eventually goes his/her own way. The only child demands a great deal of attention, has difficulty in life when he/she is not the center of attention, and becomes dependent upon the mother.

In family therapy, the Lifestyle Assessment is administered in the initial interview. The purpose is to diagnose the child's goals, evaluate parental child-rearing methods, and make specific recommendations for change.

Adlerians approach the therapeutic conference with a positive view of human nature and respect for the client's need to be in control of prevailing social forces. The therapist starts to build the relationship by creating a contract. This contract emphasizes the client's responsibility, together with the therapist, for the success of the therapeutic process.

The therapist recognizes that the client's lifestyle pattern, developed at an early age, influences an individual's way of dealing with life stresses. The main thrust of the therapy is to examine the client's lifestyle.[REC1] [REC2]The goals of Adlerian therapy are to help clients overcome discouragement, alter negative motivation and "basic mistakes", and aid in helping clients find some measure of equality with society and others

Adlerians use various techniques to fulfill the goals of the therapy. There is not a set regime or procedure; the therapist uses whatever methods are needed to accomplish these goals. This gives the therapist the freedom to work with their clients as they see fit, choosing from a variety of techniques. Some techniques include, but are not limited to, encouragement, paradoxical intention, confrontation, summarizing, interpretation of past and present family dynamics, suggestion, humor, silence, and the assignment of homework.

For more information about Adlerian psychotherapy, go to ourworld.compuserve.com/homepages/hstein.

Contributions of *Adler's* theory are:

1. The theory was a major impetus for the development of other humanistic theories.

2. The theory has influenced cognitive-behavioral theories, family therapies, and general mental health work. Currently, it is impacting emerging theories of culturally competent counseling.

The limitations of *Adler's* theory are:

1. An inability to validate the vaguely defined concepts with empirical data.

2. The oversimplification of complex human functioning.

3. It is based too heavily on a common sense perspective.

Key terms of *Adlerian* thought are:

Avoiding traps - the therapist's efforts to avoid reinforcing clients' destructive behavior patterns.

Basic Mistakes - self-defeating beliefs (such as an extreme need for security, unattainable goals and doubting one's worth) which influence the formation of one's personality.

Catching oneself - the process of the client to become more aware of self-destructive behavior, irrational thoughts, and the anticipation of events before they happen.

Convictions - the results of life experiences.

Courage - the ability to take risks.

Encouragement - the process used in therapy to help clients reach realistic goals by using all their resources, recognizing their positive traits and transforming negative traits into positive assets.

Family Constellations - "pictures" of family dynamics and relationships.

Fictional Finalism - the ideal image one sees oneself becoming; one's ultimate goal.

Holism - the viewing of one's personality as a whole.

Immediacy - dealing with the present moment in the counseling process.

Individual Psychology - the uniqueness and unity of the individual.

Individuality - the way we develop our own style of striving for competence.

Inferiority Feelings - the negative feeling one has about oneself. These feelings can be both real and imagined.

Life Tasks - the life work of all humans to attain a satisfying lifestyle.

Lifestyle - the way in which one perceives life and upon which the personality is formed.

Motivational Modification - the therapist's interest in helping clients to want to change their' negative lifestyle goals and challenging their basic negative concepts.

Paradoxical Intention - the technique that is characterized by helping the client invoke exaggerated debilitating thoughts and behaviors, helping the client accept and conquer his/her resistance, thus becoming more aware of his/her behavior and being responsible for the consequences of that behavior.

Phenomenological Orientation - the technique of the therapist that attempts to view the world from the client's point of view.

Priorities - a coping method used to obtain satisfaction in life. By pointing out a client's priorities the therapist hopes to help the client realize the feelings invoked in others and the price the client pays by clinging to these negative priorities.

Private Logic - the central psychological framework of the client; the philosophy upon which one bases one's lifestyle, including basic mistakes and faulty assumptions that often do not conform to reality.

Push-Button - a technique that teaches the client that he/she can control and their thoughts and feelings.

Social Interest - the attitude a client has regarding society; a sense of empathy and identification with the larger community.

Spitting in the Client's Soup - a technique that reduces the usefulness of a client's manipulative behavior. By pointing out the manipulation, the therapist effectively defeats the client's anticipated results of the manipulation.

Striving for Superiority - the desire to become competent and perfect; also known as the "**growth force**".

Task Setting and Commitment - the technique taught to the client to formulate realistic, attainable goals that can be revised if necessary.

BEHAVIORISM

The behavioral theories of psychological development and therapy that developed in the 1950s and 1960s were a radical protest to the psychoanalytic theories that had held sway for many years. The key figures in behaviorism were **Arnold Lazarus**, **Albert Bandura**, **Joseph Wolpe** and **Alan Kazdin**. They built on the work of learning theorists (see Skill 1.2). Contemporary behavior therapy utilizes many concepts, research methods, and treatments to account for and change behavior. In contrast to the psychoanalytic theories, behavior therapies are focused on current behavior as well as methods to change self-destructive behaviors.

Behavior theory describes the principles of learned behavior. The main goal of behavior therapy is to eliminate negative learned behaviors or self-defeating behaviors by having the client learn new, more effective and positive ways of dealing with situations that create behavior problems. The client and the therapist work together to formulate goals. In this process, they detail specific methods to address the client's self-defeating behavior. The client must have a sense of ownership regarding the goals in order to make them work.

The job of the therapist in behavior therapy is to
- make the problem clear,
- verbalize the consequences of the behavior manifested by the client,
- serve as a role model for the client,
- help formulate alternative courses of action with possible consequences,
- advocate behavior change, and provide reinforcement to the client when the behavior changes.

There[REC3] should be an objective assessment of the results of the therapy. The job of the client is to help the therapist explore the alternatives to the problematic behavior, be open to trying new strategies and be willing to take the risk of trying these new strategies outside the therapeutic session.

Although the goals of the therapy are specific and concrete, and the problems are defined, the procedures and techniques of the therapy are contingent upon the needs of each client. Therefore no set of specific techniques is used, although some methods are used more often than others. Some of these methods are relaxation, systematic desensitization, reinforcement, modeling, assertive training, multimodal therapy and self-management programs. Therapy should focus on behavior change, not on attitude change, and actions are expected to follow verbalization (in other words, practice in real life).

Contributions of *behavior* theory and therapy are:

1. The techniques are based upon empirical research. Any technique that is not effective empirically is discarded.

2. Treatment is based upon the assessment of individual needs.

3. The therapy is effective in the short-term, yielding results that can be widely applied.

4. The approaches can be used with culturally diverse client populations because of the emphasis on teaching the client about the process and the structure of the therapy.

Some of the limitations of *behavior* therapy are:

1. Success depends upon the ability to control environmental factors.

2. In institutional settings, there is a danger of imposing conformity at the expense of individual needs.

3. The therapy does not address philosophical human problems such as values and identity issues.

4. The therapist can, if desired, direct a client towards the goals of the therapist instead of the goals of the client. This may be especially true if the therapist does not agree with the client's value system.

5. Past history is not an important factor in the therapy, therefore the assumption is that past experiences and childhood traumatic events do not play a role in present behaviors.

Key terms in *behaviorism* are:

Assertive Training - Teaching skills and techniques for dealing with difficult situations in ways that are direct, firm and clear. Assertive training often challenges beliefs that accompany a lack of assertiveness and employs the technique of rehearsal.

Basic ID - an acronym for the seven major areas of personality functioning: **b**ehavior, **a**ffect, **s**ensations, **i**magery, **c**ognition, **i**nterpersonal and **d**rugs/biology. (Lazarus, 1981)

Behavior Rehearsal - a technique of trying out new behavioral approaches that can be used in real life situations.
Coaching - providing clients with general principles of how to make effective behavioral changes.

Cognitive Restructuring - the process of identifying and understanding the impact of negative behavior and thoughts, as well as learning to replace them with more realistic and appropriate actions and beliefs.

Contingency Contracting - the specific delineation of behavior to be performed, changed or discontinued, along with the rewards for the performance of these contractual items, the conditions under which these rewards are to be received, and the time limit involved.

Counterconditioning - the process of retraining problem behaviors and introducing new behaviors.

Feedback - the process of providing the client with verbal responses to behavior changes. The two parts of feedback are encouragement and praise for attempting the behavior change, and specific suggestions for making the behavior change work better.

Modeling - the process of showing new ways to do something. The therapist can help the client do this by role-playing the type of behavior that is desired. Albert Bandura has done much of the work in this area.

Multimodal Therapy - the process the therapist evokes in making an evaluation of the client's level of functioning at the beginning of the therapy, and subsequently adjusting procedures and techniques to the goals of the client. The behavior change is a function of techniques, strategies and modeling. Arnold Lazarus developed this type of therapy.

Negative Reinforcement - when the removal of an aversive stimulus is likely to increase a problem behavior.

Operant Conditioning - a concept from B.F. Skinner (a learning theorist) that says behaviors of an active organism are controlled and controllable, even without actual consequences each time.

Positive Reinforcement - a conditioning technique where an individual receives a desirable result for a positive behavior that subsequently increases the probability of that behavior reoccurring.

Progressive Relaxation - a technique employed to increase the ability of the client to control his/her stress level by gradually having the client relax.

Reinforcement - a specific response to a behavior that increases the probability of that behavior being repeated.

Self-Instructional Training/Management - strategies used to teach coping skills in problem situations such as anxiety, depression, and pain. Realistic goals are set and constantly evaluated. The consistent use of a particular strategy is essential, and support systems are important as are the use of self-reinforcement in order to achieve success.

Self-Monitoring - the process of observing one's behavior patterns and interactions in social situations.

Social Learning Theory - a theory originated by Alfred Bandura. The theory holds that behavior is understood by taking into consideration the social conditions under which learning occurs as well as individual psychological factors.

Systematic Desensitization - the process of teaching a client to become less sensitized to a particular stimulus, thereby reducing anxiety. The techniques consist of relaxation exercises combined with an imagined series of progressively more anxiety-producing situations. It was developed by Joseph Wolpe and is based upon the principles of classical conditioning.

Technical Eclecticism - the process of using different techniques from different therapies to achieve behavior change; the results is; flexibility in the therapeutic process.

COGNITIVE-BEHAVIOR THERAPY

In cognitive-behavior therapy clients explore reasons for their behavior by understanding their thoughts. They are also encouraged to look at the ramifications of their behavior on themselves, others, and the environment in which they live and function.

One of the major approaches in the field of cognitive-behavior therapy is *Rational-Emotive Therapy*, **also referred to as Rational-Emotive Behavior Therapy (REBT). Albert Ellis** founded of Rational-Emotive Therapy and is effectively the grandfather of all cognitive-behavior therapies. He believed that the concepts of insight and awareness into childhood events did not result in the resolution of present emotional dysfunction. He also theorized that the connection between the past and the present was not explored fully in psychoanalytic theories.

The key concept in RET holds that even though emotional malfunction is rooted in childhood disturbances, individuals continue to reinforce their irrational and illogical thinking. Emotional problems are the result of irrational beliefs that need to be challenged in order for the individual to resolve the emotional maladjustment.

The **A-B-C** approach to personality is the basis of RET therapy: A=activating event, B=belief system, C=consequences. RET stresses action and practice in combating irrational and self-delusional ideas. The thinking and belief systems of the client are considered the basis for all personal problems. RET techniques include directed, time-limited, structured approaches for treating depression, anxiety, and phobic behavior. Further developments of cognitive-behavior theory are Aaron Beck's cognitive theory and Donald Meichenbaum's cognitive-behavior modification theory.

Donald Meichenbaum's cognitive-behavior theory has three phases. Clients are instructed to monitor their own behavior in order to identify negative thoughts and feelings. This is called the conceptual phase. The next phase is rehearsal, where the client creates a new internal system by substituting positive thoughts and feelings. In the application phase, the client applies more effective coping skills to real life situations. Focusing on the client's inner speech is a technique that is used in cognitive-behavior modification theory.

Similarly, **Aaron Beck** emphasized the assumption that clients' conversations with themselves play a major role in their behavior. He theorized that the way people feel and behave is based one the way they view their experiences. The therapy is short-term, active, focused and insightful. Beck's concept of automatic thoughts is the idea that certain events trigger emotional responses. The goal of the therapy is to help clients recognize and discard self-defeating thinking and correct erroneous beliefs. It has been applied particularly to the treatment of depression.

The techniques used in all cognitive-behavioral therapies are derivative of the above theorists and are tailored to the needs of the client. Any method that works may be used, though there is a bias towards approaches with empirical validation.

Cognitive techniques include disputing irrational beliefs, homework, humor and the changing of language to a more positive approach. *Emotive techniques* include imagery, role-playing and shame attacking procedures. *Behavioral techniques* include operant conditioning, self management and modeling. RET is directive, persuasive and confrontational in contrast to cognitive therapy which emphasizes dialogue to discover misconceptions.

Contributions of *cognitive-behavior* therapy are as follows:

1. Counseling tends to be brief and outcome-focused.

2. Practice and experimenting with new behaviors is emphasized.

3. The therapy stresses the clients' ability to control his/her experience of the world.

4. It is easily used with clients who are action-oriented and willing to accept responsibility for their difficulties.

5. The therapy can be effectively employed in crisis situations.

Limitations of *cognitive-behavior* therapy are as follows:

1. The underlying reasons for irrational beliefs is not explored, leaving the client open to incorporate additional different irrational beliefs into their belief system.

2. The dialogue aspect of the therapy does not lend itself to working with clients of low intelligence.

3. There is the danger of the therapist imposing his/her views on the client with the potential for psychological harm.

4. Emotional issues are not explored which may limit the effectiveness of the therapy in the long run.

Some of the key terms of *cognitive-behavioral* theory and therapy are:

A-B-C Model - the construct stating that one's problems do not originate from events but from the beliefs one holds about those events. Changing one's beliefs is the best way to change negative feelings.

Arbitrary Inferences - the distorted view of making conclusions without the basis of supporting and relevant evidence; part of Aaron Beck's cognitive therapy.

Automatic Thoughts - ideas (usually outside one's awareness) triggered by a particular event that lead to emotional reactions.

Cognitive Errors - misconceptions and wrong assumptions on the part of the client.

Cognitive Homework - the process used to help a client learn to deal with anxiety and to challenge irrational thinking.

Cognitive Restructuring - the process of replacing negative thoughts with positive thoughts and beliefs.

Cognitive Therapy - a type of therapy focused on changing negative behavior by changing false thinking and beliefs.

Collaborative Empiricism - a concept from Aaron Beck's cognitive therapy that views the client as capable of making objective interpretations of his/her behavior, along with the collaboration of the therapist.

Coping Skills Program - a set of procedures to help clients deal with stressful situations by changing their thinking.

Disputational Method - a method taught to clients in RET to help them challenge irrational beliefs.

Distortion of Reality - inaccurate thinking causing one to act irrationally, emotionally, and subjectively.

Internal Dialogue/Inner Speech - the process used to recognize irrational thoughts.

Irrational Belief - an unreasonable thought leading to emotional problems.

Labeling and Mislabeling - the distorted view of basing one's identity on imperfections and mistakes made in the past.

Musturbation - the word used by Albert Ellis to describe beliefs grounded in *musts, shoulds, and oughts;* a rigid and absolute way of thinking.

Overgeneralization - the distorted process of forming rigid beliefs based upon a single event and then applying them to subsequent events.

Personalization - the tendency for individuals to relate events to themselves when there is no basis for this connection.

Polarized Thinking - a cognitive error of based on an all-or–nothing framework. There are no gray areas in polarized thinking.

Rationality - a way of thinking that will help us attain our goals.

Role-playing - the process of helping a client work through irrational beliefs by practicing new behaviors.

Selective Abstraction - the distorted view of forming conclusions based on an isolated detail of an event.

Self-Instructional Therapy - the concept that the self-talk an individual indulges in directly relates to the things they do in every day life. The therapy consists of training the client to modify self-talk, a form of cognitive restructuring or cognitive behavior modification developed by Donald Meichenbaum.

Shame-Attacking Exercises - a technique of RET encouraging the individual to do things about which they feel shame without believing they are foolish or without becoming embarrassed

Stress-Inoculation Training - a cognitive-behavior modification technique aimed at giving the client the coping tools to restructure the thoughts that lead to stress, and to rehearse the behavior changes in order to solve the emotional problems caused by stressful situations.

EXISTENTIAL THERAPY

The evolution of existential therapy developed as a reaction to the theories of psychoanalysis and behaviorism. Existential theory differs from the psychodynamic and behavior theories in their fundamental presumptions about the nature of human beings. Psychodynamic theories are based upon a deterministic view of human nature; they see personal freedom controlled by irrational actions, past occurrences, and the unconscious. The behaviorists believe freedom is restricted by societal forces.

Existentialists believe the early theorists did not take into account all aspects of human nature. By concentrating on external objective factors, the psychodynamic theorists and the behaviorists ignored the internal frame of reference and subjective experiences of the individual. Existentialists concern themselves with questions of freedom, responsibility and choice, and the meaning of reaching one's full potential. This philosophical basis suggests people must create their own meaning through their choices in a world that is fundamentally meaningless and lonely; the individual must explore what it means to be fully human.

The assumption is that we are free and therefore responsible for our actions and the results of those actions and choices. We are the "authors of our lives" and are not the victims of circumstances because we have the freedom to change those circumstances. See www.existentialpsychotherapy.net for more information.

Some of the early European existentialists were **Ludwig Binswanger**, **Karl Jaspers**, **Medard Boss** and **Viktor Frankl**. Contemporary figures are **Rollo May** and **Irvin Yalom**. Their work is based upon the work of philosophers Dostoyevsky, Heidegger, Nietzsche, Sartre and Buber.

Viktor Frankl expounded the theory of logotherapy, which literally means "healing through reason" (logic). In developing this approach, Frankl was influenced by the earlier European existentialists. Logotherapy is designed to help people find meaning in life through their experiences.

Irvin Yalom wrote Existential Psychotherapy, a central text in the field of existential psychotherapy. In it, he addresses the core issues that make up the existential theory: isolation, meaninglessness, freedom and death within the context of the therapeutic relationship and process.

Rollo May is responsible for converting the European philosophy of existentialism into American theory and practice. He focuses on the subjective aspects of the therapy and believes that freedom and responsibility go hand in hand, with freedom requiring us to accept responsibility for who we become.

This theory requires an intellectual and philosophical approach on the part of the therapist. Existential-based therapy is relationship-oriented, experiential and philosophical. It does not have a set regime of techniques but allows for incorporation of techniques from other therapies. The general approach is to focus upon four major concerns of human existence: freedom, isolation, death and meaninglessness.

The basic goals of existential therapy are to help clients become aware they are free to make choices to improve their experience of daily life. Clients are encouraged to see past and future choices, to accept the responsibility of their choices, to recognize the factors that hinder their freedom to choose, and to experience an authentic existence.

There are six concepts to which existential therapists ascribe. They are:

1. **We are capable of self-awareness**. The expansion of this awareness, a basic goal of the therapy, is to increase our perception of the freedom to choose and to act on those choices.

2. **We are free beings and must accept the responsibility of that freedom** to decide our own fate. Although we did not choose to be in this world, how we live here and what we do with our lives are our own choices. Each choice we make creates who we are. Whatever the set of circumstances, it is our attitude that determines how we approach a situation and how we survive it.

3. **In preserving our uniqueness, we know who we are** by our relations and interactions with others. Our awareness of this individuality makes us better able to lead an authentic life style.

4. **The meaning of our lives and existence are always in a state of fluidity** as we continue to create ourselves through our actions. These actions are the result of our own choices and we are not victims of forces beyond our control.

5. **Anxiety is a normal state**. It is part of the human condition, an emotional recognition of one's vulnerability and the responsibility of choosing in an uncertain world without any guarantees. Anxiety is the result of a person's awareness of their aloneness. It is not a sick condition, but rather a growth enhancer to motivate us to change conditions that have become intolerable.

6. **Awareness of death** is a human condition that gives meaning to living. Being aware of our ultimate death is the impetus for us to live our lives to the fullest. Life has meaning because it is not forever. The question is not how long we live, as we all will eventually die, but how we live that life, which creates meaning for our every day existence.

The focus of *existential* therapy is:

1. To confront the reality of being in the world alone and facing the anxiety of this isolation,

2. To understand one's subjective world,

3. To revise the assumptions arising from one's subjectivity, and

4. To make choices that lead to the living of an authentic life.

The approach is not based on curing sickness or solving immediate problems, but on utilizing the inherent knowledge of life experiences to live a fuller and more authentic existence.

Contributions of *existential* theory are:

1. The client-therapist relationship is based upon the humanity of the individual.

2. The theory addresses the major concerns of healthy individuals as they go through life cycles by concentrating on issues important to attaining life satisfaction.

3. The model allows for the inclusion of many other modalities within the larger philosophical framework provided by existential theory. In other words, psychodynamic explorations and cognitive-behavior techniques may be employed as part of the therapy.

The limitations of *existential* theory are:

1. A lack of a systematic procedure.

2. The concepts can be difficult to comprehend, and require a particular orientation and effort on the part of the therapist.

3. There is no scientific research done on the model.

4. Lower functioning clients, clients in crisis who need immediate direction, and nonverbal clients may not be able to benefit from a philosophical and intellectual approach to problem solving.

Some of the key terms of *existential* therapy are:

Aloneness - a natural human condition from which we can derive strength to become free. When mastered we will have the ability to stand beside others to lend them support in their own aloneness.

Anxiety - the experience we have when we realize we are not immortal, that we face constant choices in an uncertain world, and when we realize we are fundamentally alone.

Authenticity - the ability to be true to our own ideas of a meaningful existence and to accept responsibility for the conditions of our lives, a result of the choices we have made.

Authorship - the concept that we create our own life situations, problems and destinies.

Awareness - the freedom to choose and act on our choices.

"Bad Faith" - the inauthenticity of not accepting the freedom to take responsibility for our own actions.

Existential Guilt - the result of the feelings we have when we permit others to shape our lives and make our choices.

Existential Neurosis - feelings of despair resulting from a failure to make our own choices.

Existential Vacuum - a condition of emptiness and depression that results from a meaningless lifestyle.

Existentialism - a philosophical movement that stresses individual responsibility for creating one's own ways of behaving, thinking, and feeling.

Freedom - the ability to be responsible for our own destiny and to be accountable for our own actions.

Logotherapy - a branch of existential therapy that challenges clients to search for meaning in life; developed by Viktor Frankl.

Meaninglessness - the fact that there is no inherent meaning in living, and it is up to us to create our own system of meaning.

Phenomenology - a method used in therapy to utilize subjective experiences as a therapeutic focus that is used in many existing theories.

Restricted Existence - the condition of one's functioning with a limited awareness of self and the inability to define the true nature of the problem.
"The Courage to Be" - our ability to live to our fullest, rather than living in within the constraints of what others expect; also, the ability to accept limitations and confront the feelings of emptiness that comes when we are to make new choices.

PERSON - CENTERED THERAPY

The founder of person-centered therapy was **Carl Rogers**. In the early 1940's Rogers created the "nondirective counseling" approach. Later he was involved in advocating for the encounter group movement and was a pioneer in the humanistic approach to counseling. He was opposed to the therapist acting as the expert whose advice dictated what the client needed to do to be well. He felt clients contain the ability to become a more fully functioning "self-actualized" person. Rogers believed all people have a "formative tendency" or inner energy which propels us towards fulfillment and self-actualization.

This theory rests upon the assumption that individuals have internal resources to work toward wholeness and self-actualization if properly supported and encouraged. Person-centered therapists believe clients can move forward constructively on their own. The focus is on understanding the feelings and thoughts expressed by the client from the vantage point of the client's subjective world. The theory emphasizes the personality and attitude of the therapist/facilitator, rather than concentrating on techniques (although the skills of active listening and reflecting are most often used).

This approach is a "way of being rather than a way of doing." Positive attitudes and behaviors on the part of the therapist create a climate of growth that not only reaches the client but which surrounds the client. This helps create an aura of "personal power," or the awareness of one's own feelings, needs and values, that is subsequently sensed by others and facilitates effective functioning.

The therapist's role is to create an atmosphere of empathy, acceptance, warmth and caring an environment of unconditional positive regard. The success of the therapy depends upon the therapist maintaining this climate as the major tool for facilitating positive outcomes for the therapy. In this environment, the client begins to drop defensive attitudes and concentrates more on meaningful goals, leading to positive and appropriate actions. Eventually the client uses the learning acquired in the safe environment of the therapy to apply to relationships outside the therapeutic setting. The focus is on experiencing and perceiving the immediate moment as an opportunity for change

Three characteristics of the therapist lend themselves to creating the atmosphere needed for client self-actualization:

Genuineness - the goal of person-centered therapists is to be aware of their feelings and attitudes, their shortcomings and their humility. They do not hide behind a professional demeanor, but align themselves with the person being counseled.

Unconditional Positive Regard - a positive, nonjudgmental acceptance and caring attitude on the part of the therapist.

Empathic Understanding - the ability to accurately sense the feelings and meanings of the client and to express these feeling and meanings so the client understands the therapist is truly in attuned to the client.

For more information about this approach, literature and training options, contact the Association for the Development of the Person Centered Approach at www.adpca.org.

The contributions of *person-centered* therapy are:

1. The relevance of the therapist as a person breaks from more traditional forms of therapy and offers a more accessible model for some clients.

2. It is a relationship-centered therapy instead of a technique-centered therapy.

3. While the therapist assumes responsibility for creating an environment that is conducive to the client's success the responsibility for the direction of the therapy lies with the client.
4. The theory concentrates on a person's need to account for his/her inner experiences and has relied upon research to validate the concepts, practices and approach.

5. This theory inherently respects individual differences and therefore is very amenable to culturally competent therapy.

The limitation of the *person-centered* approach is dependent upon the personal limitations of the therapists themselves. Limitations may include the following:

1. There can be lack of genuine empathy. The therapist may hold stereotypes about certain clients that make it difficult for a therapist to have positive regard, warmth, and acceptance for them.

2. The inability of the therapist to practice appropriate self-disclosure can be a problem. A person-centered approach requires that the therapist have the capacity to self-disclose, but also maintain boundaries. Finding this balance and being truly genuine requires a high degree of self-awareness and self-control on the part of the therapist.

3. Temperamentally, a therapist may not be best suited to the person-centered approach. The therapist may not listen well, or too readily makes assumptions. Further, the therapist may be anxious to solve problems rather than understand the problem to be solved, and have the capacity to allow the process of change to unfold.

4. The therapist may lack the belief that the client can change behavior, thus creating an atmosphere conducive to failure.

5. Person-centered therapy is not effective with people in crises situations who are looking for immediate problem solving strategies.

Some of the key terms of *person-centered* therapy are:

Accurate Empathic Understanding - the therapist's ability to sense the client's inner world (i.e., the client's subjective experience).

Congruence - a state in which self-experiences are accurately represented by self-concept; there is a matching of inner experience with external expressions; also refers to the genuineness of the therapist.

Facilitator - the role the therapist takes in person-centered therapy.

Genuineness - a state of authenticity resulting from self-analysis and a willingness to accept the truth of who one is.

Humanistic Psychology - a movement emphasizing freedom, choice, values, growth, self-actualization, spontaneity, creativity, play, humor and psychological health.

Nondirective Counseling - the type of counseling that assumes the client is the one who knows what is best and should not be in a passive role. This results in the therapist permitting the client to lead the counseling instead of the therapist doing the leading.

Incongruence - the discrepancy between self-concept and ideal self-concept. Incongruence usually results in anxiety, which can serve as a clue to the existence of a problem.

Internal Source of Evaluation - the process of looking to oneself for answers to problems.

Personal Power - the sense of strength that comes from knowing oneself and one's ability to mobilize energy. The therapist's ability to access his/her own personal power facilitates the client's development of personal power, rather than for controlling other people.

Self-Actualization - an inner growth force leading to the development of one's potential and the basis of people being trusted to resolve their own problems in a therapeutic relationship.

Therapeutic Conditions - the necessary conditions of the therapeutic relationship that allow the client to change. These conditions include therapist congruence, unconditional positive regard and accurate empathic understanding.

Unconditional Positive Regard - the acceptance of the client's right to all their feelings without conditions imposed by the therapist.

GESTALT THERAPY

Frederick Perls is considered the founder of Gestalt therapy. **Erving** and **Miriam Polster** were key figures in the development of Perls' concepts. The theory stresses the "here and now" and focuses upon bringing together the parts of the personality that are not integrated into the whole person. It also focuses on the "what and how" of behavior as well as the role unfinished business from the past plays in preventing the individual from adequately functioning in the present. The most frequent cause of unfinished business is resentment. Other sources of unfinished business are avoidance, guilt, anger grief and other feelings that remain unresolved.

Perls' theory includes the following five layers of neurosis:

1. The phony layer: acting as others wish us to act, playing games.
2. The phobic layer: avoiding the confrontation of who we really are.
3. The impasse layer: the sense of deadness or foreboding doom.
4. The implosive layer: fully experiencing our deadness.
5. The explosive layer: the releasing of phony roles to experience a feeling of relief.

Gestalt therapy is, in part, derived from existentialist therapy. Some of the major concepts of the therapy are:

- accepting responsibility for being in the here-and-now
- becoming aware of the present moment (itself a therapeutic process)
- facing the issues of avoidance

- dealing with impasses
- dealing with unfinished business from the past

Clients are expected to be active in their own therapy, to do their own interpreting, and to grow through personal contact. Gestalt therapists emphasize the awareness of personal contact at our boundaries with the world via our senses. This awareness is necessary for growth and change. The client resists contact by a variety of methods such as introjection, projection and retroflection.

The goals of the therapy are:

- To challenge the client to develop methods of self-support in order to replace the environmental support system presently in effect
- To become more aware of the "here and now" and the self
- To recognize the parts of the self that have been denied
- To assume ownership and responsibility for this denial.

The focus is not on the techniques of the therapy, but on the therapist as a person and the role of helping the client make his/her own interpretations. The techniques of the therapy are to intensify direct experience in the moment. . Clients role-play and experiment with different scenarios to gain greater awareness of their inner conflicts and to intensify their experiences. In the role-playing aspects of the therapy, the therapist asks the client to play out all the roles experienced in a dream sequence, for example, in order for the client to better understand the dream. An "empty chair" may be placed in front of the client as a device to facilitate the expression of feelings.

More information about Gestalt theory and therapy, including access to key journals in the field, is available www.gestalt.org.

Some of the contributions of *Gestalt* theory are:

1. This approach can de-emphasize the intellectualization of the client's problems and focus on here-and-now experience of interpersonal contact.

2. It lends itself to brief therapy due to the intensity of the experiences of the client.

3. It utilizes dreams and unfinished business from the past in order to understand current problems.

4. The theory can be applied to group counseling, school and classroom problems, and workshop settings as well as individual counseling sessions.

Some limitations of *Gestalt* theory are:

1. It does not give much credence to cognitive factors, nor does it emphasize the importance of empathy and positive regard for the client.

2. It can become a technique-oriented theory with the potential of the therapist misdirecting the course of the therapy for the sake of the techniques.

3. The therapist can slip into autocracy, assuming the role of director rather than facilitator.

4. There is a lack of empirical research to validate the theory.

Some key terms in *Gestalt* therapy are:

Aboutism - the speaking of an incident in the past in contrast to speaking of the same incident in the present.

Avoidance - a technique used by clients to keep from facing unfinished business, from feeling uncomfortable emotions and from having to make changes in their life.

Awareness - the process of exploring one's thinking, feelings and actions.

Blaming Games - a technique used by the client to avoid taking responsibility for his/her growth, to avoid staying in the "now", and to prevent themselves from the pain of experiencing the "here and now".

Boundary Disturbance/Resistance to Contact - a technique practiced by individuals who attempt to control their environment; it can have both negative and positive consequences.

Confluence - the blurring of awareness of the difference between oneself and the environment.

Confrontation - the act of becoming aware of differences between verbal and nonverbal expressions, feelings and actions, and thoughts and actions.

Contact boundary – the interface or point of contact between an individual and the world around him or her, including other people.

Deflection - the process of distraction or inattention, making it difficult to sustain contact.

Dichotomy/Polarity - a split in which a person experiences opposing forces.

Explosive Layer - the mode of releasing the pretenses of phony roles in order to achieve a sense of relief and release.

Here-and-Now Awareness - the ability of the client to realize what s/he is experiencing in the present moment.

Impasse - the point at which we are stuck in a stage of less than full maturation. This may be accompanied by feelings of deadness or impending doom and a wish to avoid threatening feelings.

Implosive Level - the mode in which we allow ourselves to fully experience our deadness or inauthenticity. This leads to the chance to make contact with our genuine self.

Introjection - the acceptance of others' beliefs and standards without analyzing, assimilating and internalizing them.

Modes of Defense - the five layers of neurotic avoidance: the phony, the phobic, the impasse, the implosive and the explosive.

Phobic Layer - the mode of the avoiding of the emotional pain that comes with recognizing our real selves.

Phony Layer - the mode of reacting to others in stereotypical and inauthentic ways, in other words, playing games.

"Play the Projection" - a technique used to help clients see how they project onto others things they do not want to recognize in themselves.

Projection - disowning parts of ourselves by blaming them on the environment.

Resistance - defenses developed which prevent fully experiencing the present.

Retroflection - turning back to ourselves what we would like to do or have done to others.

Unfinished Business - unexpressed feelings (such as resentment, guilt, anger and grief) from childhood that are presently preventing effective psychological functioning; needless emotional garbage.

REALITY THERAPY

William Glasser developed the concept of reality therapy in the 1950s and 1960s. Originally, the approach emphasized individual responsibility. In the 1980s Glasser expanded this concept to a theory of control. Control theory emphasizes doing and thinking. The theory attempts to explain why and how people behave from the point of view of the subjective internal perception of their world. Glasser posits that the purpose of behaving the way we do is to eliminate the discrepancy between what we presently have and what we want.

The theory is also based upon the assertion that we are in charge of our lives, we choose our forms of behavior, and that behavior is intended to increase self-esteem and a sense of belonging, and to attain power and freedom. The therapy focuses on exploring ways to effectively manage our world so we can get what we want without hurting others in the process.

Reality therapy does not dwell on the past, the unconscious, the role of insight, or take into consideration the process of transference. Its goal is to help client clients acquire skills to take control of their lives, better cope with life's demands, and solve present day problems. The purpose is to achieve a satisfying, effective existence. The challenge in therapy is to examine how people are presently functioning in order to improve that functioning. The therapy is short-term and designed to help people develop a "success identity" by meeting the four psychological needs of belonging, power, freedom, and fun.

The therapist's relationship with the client is one of concern, support, and warmth. While the therapist is involved with clients in a positive way, he/she does not accept excuses for inappropriate behavior, and continuously prods and pushes to help the client accept reality and responsibility for his/her actions. The client is expected to take responsibility for deciding what goals to pursue and commit to those goals, to make value judgments about his/her current behavior, to plan a specific course of action for future success, and to make a commitment to carry out these plans in every day life.

The *WDEP model* is the procedure applied in the practice of reality-therapy.

W=Wants - Through questioning by the therapist, clients are able to express their wants, needs and perceptions of what is happening in every day life.

D=Doing - The therapist explores what clients are doing and what direction they are taking in their behavior to obtain those wants and needs.

E=Evaluation - The therapist encourages clients to evaluate their behavior patterns that help or do not help obtain those needs and wants.

P=Planning and Commitment - The therapist invites and encourages clients to plan for behavior change and commit to that change.

Glasser originally used his therapy in working with youthful offenders but the theory of control has been successfully used in individual, marital, family and group counseling, in alcohol and drug abuse clinics, and with students, teachers and administrators.

Contributions of *reality* therapy are the following:

1. Clients are responsible for evaluating and changing their behavior.

2. The client is the catalyst in making specific plans, forming contracts for action and evaluating the success of these actions.

3. The emphasis is upon accountability. No excuses for failure are accepted but blame and punishment for not carrying out the stated changes are avoided. The focus instead is on what prevented the client from carrying out the plan of action and the readjustment to a more reasonable plan of action.

4. There is a structure to evaluate the degree and nature of the changes effected.

5. It is a short-term, clear and easily understood therapy that is applicable to different situations and clients, some of whom may not usually be receptive to other therapy approaches.

Limitations of *reality* therapy are:

1. Consideration is not given to feelings, the unconscious, and the past.

2. The influence of the culture and environment of the client is not taken into consideration when looking for alternatives to the maladjusted behavior. The focus is on the symptoms. The origin of the behavior is not taken into account.

3. There is a lack of research on reality therapy to establish its effectiveness.

Key terms of this approach are:

Autonomy - the acceptance of responsibility and the taking control of the direction of one's life; a state of maturity

Commitment - the ability on the part of the client to continue with a reasonable plan to effect the desired change

TEACHER CERTIFICATION STUDY GUIDE

Control Theory - a theory of why people act the way they do; the internal motivation to master one's own world.

Involvement - the role of the therapist with the client in reality therapy, a vital part of establishing a relationship with the client.

Paining Behaviors - the manifestation of pain symptoms, such as depression, to refocus the problem on the symptoms instead of the behavior.

Perceived World - one's subjective world.

Picture Album - the perceived reality of the client formulated to meet their psychological needs.

Positive Addiction - the acts performed to gain psychological strength such as physical activity and meditation.

Responsibility - the dependable manner in which we satisfy our needs without interfering with the rights of others.

Success Identity - the state of self-esteem needed to fulfill the behaviors deemed necessary for attaining a more satisfying life experience. The end result of attaining a success identity is that the individual is able to give and receive love, has a sense of self-worth, and possesses the strength to create a satisfying life.

Total Behavior - the blend of the sum of all our activities that forms our personality and the person we have become.

Value Judgment - the evaluation of current behaviors to determine their value.

WDEP System - the abbreviation for the components of reality therapy: the identification of **w**ants, the **d**irection of behavior, the **e**valuation of self, and the **p**lan for change.

SOLUTION-FOCUSED THERAPY

Solution-focused therapy was initially developed by **de Shazer** and **Berg** in recent years. The theory is based on work by various family therapists and the work of **Milton Erickson.** It is considered a brief therapy model, sometimes only comprising one session, which lends itself well to many guidance situations.

This model asserts that when clients come to counseling they have a picture of what they would like to be different about their lives and often have the answers to their problems. By providing a constructivist process, the counselor facilitates the process by helping the client in defining the problem, identifying viable solutions, and planning for working towards the desired behavior or reality. The core of solution-focused therapy lies not in the "why" but the "how." Theorists of this orientation argue that the past cannot be changed, so why not focus on how the client wants the future to be more satisfying?

Walter & Peller identified the following guides to making therapeutic choices:

1. Don't bother with what works. Make a determination to do more of it. Success can only be maximized.

2. Build on the small successes.

3. Experimentation is encouraged. Just because something has not been solved in the past it does not mean what was tried is the only possible solution.

4. Change is about the "here and now." Make the most of the current session.

A major focus of the work involves the counselor asking a range of questions to help draw out possible solutions. The solution-focused counselor first asks about the goal the client is hoping to achieve and is not dissuaded or discouraged it the client replies, "I don't know." The counselor empathically reframes these initial questions in order to solicit a goal. Effective goal-setting is critical to the success of solution-focused therapy.

The counselor facilitates the client's desire for change by asking what would be different if, after a night of sleep, the undesired behavior or situation had changed. The client is then engaged in a creative process of constructing a vision of positive behavioral difference or success. The counselor uses the vision as a framework upon which a solution will be defined.

Other questions are used to help the client identify desirable outcomes. The counselor's job is to reflect back the answers in ways that help clients better understand their strengths and skills as well as the nature of the problem. By the end of the session, the counselor assigns the solution as homework to practice in the time between the current and next session. The success of the applied solution can be reviewed in a following session, if there is one.

Contributions of *solution-focused* therapy:

1. Therapeutic work is accomplished with relatively few sessions.

2. Counseling is focused on the reality of the client and is not dependent on the interpretation of the client about past experience.

3. Clients are empowered to make change by what they envision of themselves through magical thinking.

4. The work is solution-focused, not problem-focused.

Limitations of *solution-focused* therapy:

1. Long-term and personality-based issues cannot be resolved by finding a solution.

2. Problems are over-generalized and oversimplified without in-depth consideration to the level of impact on the client's reality.

3. More empirical research needs to be conducted.

Some key terms of *solution-focused* therapy:

Coping questions - a series of questions the counselor uses to help the client identify previously unrecognized coping skills and strengths.

Exception-seeking question – a way to help clients discover the times when the identified problem does NOT trouble them.

Miracle question - a technique wherein the counselor encourages the client to imagine what it would be like if the problem he/she is facing were suddenly gone.

Scaling questions - a tool where clients rate the problem in varying degrees of severity in order to set goals and facilitate change.

SKILL 1.2 Counseling Theories in Relation to Personality, Learning and Human Development Theory

Counseling theories and counselors deal with behavior. Most often the behavior exhibited by people in need of counseling is abnormal, disturbing or problematic in some way. I It is the work of the counselor to help malfunctioning individuals bring their behavior under control. Maladaptive behaviors are expressed is through the personality of each individual. Therefore, change through counseling often involved both behavior change and, to some extent, personality change. These individuals manifest behavior disorders through their personalities.

Since the goal of counseling is behavior change, and to a certain extent, personality change, the counselor deals both with counseling theories of behavior change and personality change. Although different counseling theories deal with behavior change in different ways, the ultimate goal of counseling is to affect behavior by changing attitudes, feelings, perceptions, and values which to a large extent impact ones' personality. In addition, since learning is a form of behavior change, counseling is concerned with learning new ways of changing inappropriate and ineffective behavior.

The discussion of counseling theories implies the involvement of personality and learning theory. In effect, every theory of counseling has theories of personality and learning that are implied or specified as components of the larger theory. Some theories also address concepts or stages of human development. However, there is not necessarily a theory of counseling for every theory of personality or learning.

Most approaches to counseling have not emerged from learning theories although both learning and counseling concern themselves with behavior change. In addition, counseling theories have not been evaluated by applying a theory of learning. Since there is no single theory of learning, it is not possible to apply a specific learning theory to a specific counseling theory, as many learning theories can be incorporated into a specific counseling theory.

Learning theories are varied; they include the functionalists, the associationists and the cognitive developmentalists. The study of consciousness within the context of the environment, instead of studying consciousness as an isolated element, was the main contribution of the functionalist theorists **Edward Thorndike**, **B.F. Skinner** and **C.L. Hull** to learning theory. They opposed the introspective techniques of psychoanalytic approaches because it did not explore the relationship with other elements in the person's environment. The functionalists insisted that mental function be studied in relationship to the world surrounding the individual.

The associationist theorists, **Ivan Pavlov** and **William Estes** believed that experience or recall of one object builds upon and causes the recall of other objects related to or associated with that object. This is based on the theories of Aristotle. Associationistic theorists believe that living organisms' responses to environmental stimuli are governed by the sensory, response, and central nervous systems which consist of innate circuitry and memories of past experiences. The response of organisms is therefore dependent upon associating past memories with present stimuli. This theory applied to a learning theory explains how infants expand their sphere of knowledge.

Cognitive theorists, **Jean Piaget**, **Edward Tolman**, **Albert Bandura** and **Donald Norman**, assign a prominent role to mental processes. The process of learning depends upon information received and the processing of that information which in turn depends upon mental processes, past experiences or behaviors, and present environmental factors. The person, the environment and behavior are interdependent. Faulty cognitive processes develop from inaccurate perceptions, overgeneralization or from incomplete or erroneous information.

In addressing the relationship of learning, personality, and counseling theories to human development theory, it is helpful to understand the stages of human development as outlined by Jean Piaget. Development is defined as *the adaptive, orderly, changes experienced by the human organism from birth to death*. The child grows cognitively, socially, physically, and morally, gradually and at different rates. These four different types of growth and development impact on the learning process and the behavior patterns of the child.

Piaget studied how we organize knowledge at different times in our lives. He identified four stages of cognitive development. These are:

1. Sensorimotor Stage - From birth to two years. Development is based upon reflex; information is gained through the senses; the child begins to understand the concept of permanence, and begins to develop *problem solving behavior* through trial and error.

2. Pre-operational Stage - From ages two to seven years. The child starts to develop the ability to share experiences with others, uses symbols and shows rudimentary logical mental operations. The child has yet to develop the concept of *conservation,* the ability to understand that certain properties of an object do not change even though their appearance has changed. The concept of *centration* is the child's logic at this stage. This is the ability to focus on only one aspect of the properties of an object and not being able to understand that an object can have multiple properties without inherently changing. *Reversibility* at this stage is the inability of the child to back up and rethink a problem. The child can only respond to perceived appearances.

3. Concrete Operational Stage - From ages seven to eleven. At this stage the child understands the concepts of conservation, centration, and reversibility; masters the operations of classification, the identification of characteristics and serialization, and is capable of inferences. The child can now respond to inferred reality or facts.

4. Formal Operational Stage - From ages eleven to adult. At this stage the child develops and refines the capability of abstract thinking, can deal with hypothetical situations and exercises higher order thinking such as synthesis and evaluation.

One limitation of Piaget's theory is the fact that he did not consider the effect of culture and the social environment on children's development. Further, any given child's development is not as tidy and consistent as theory and therefore does not always fit into ordered patterns.

The differences in children and their rate of development are influenced by the experiences they have and the environment or culture in which they live. Their socioeconomic status, gender, language acquisition, cognitive ability and heredity are all factors in an individual's uniqueness that influence their behavior and how they see their world.

Current theories of cognitive development focus on the concept that humans develop according to various information processing mechanism that are specific to different areas of learning and growth. This is called domain specificity. These theorists argue that information processing is grounded in evolutionary adaptation. A leading proponent of this approach in relation to language acquisition is **Noam Chomsky**.

Basic Milestones in Physical and Motor Development

The majority of physical and motor growth occurs prior to five years of age. The primary exception to this is the transition at preadolescence (approximately ages 9-12) into puberty. Hormonal shifts and ongoing physical growth bring children into adolescence and physical maturity.

The key physical and motor developmental milestones for school-age children and adolescents are noted below.

Ages 6-8:

- Growth slows but remains steady.
- Body proportions change, with legs getting longer.
- Less body fat and more muscle develops, with an increase in overall strength.
- Fine motor skills are enhanced, though muscle coordination is still uneven.
- Permanent teeth come in, sometimes causing crowding if the mouth has not developed enough.

Ages 9-12:

- Significant body changes as puberty approaches: weight gain, pubic and body hair, increased sweating, oily skin, genital development.
- Some children experience joint pain as a result of growth spurts.
- Girls generally develop sooner: their hips widen, breasts start to emerge, menstruation begins.
- Boys enter preadolescence later and their growth changes last longer.

Ages 13-17:

- Puberty is reached; the adolescent is physically mature.
- Girls reach their adult height by age 17; boys continue to add height into their 20s.

The following websites provide detailed information about developmental milestones: **www.ces.ncsu.edu/depts/fcs/human.html, www.littleab.com/ABcare/develoment.html, and www.education.com/reference/ontrack/.**

Individual and Developmental Variations

Any given child's developmental path is not as tidy and consistent as theory and therefore does not always fit into ordered patterns. This is an important concept when considering theories, stages and developmental milestones. Stage theories and lists of developmental milestones need to be considered markers to guide the observer, not absolute standards within which all children will neatly fit.

The differences in children and their rate of development are influenced by the experiences they have and the environment or culture in which they live. Basic differences in caregiver style and availability, the quality of physical nutrition, and the presence or lack of trauma and violence in the environment all impact children's development. Socioeconomic status, gender, language acquisition, basic cognitive ability and heredity are other factors that influence children's development, behavior and their perspective on the world, as do ethnicity and race.

School counselors and other professionals need to be aware of developmental theories and milestones. Such knowledge provides a background against which they are better able to determine if a child or adolescent is developmentally delayed or needs assistance in reaching his or her full potential. However, the uniqueness of each individual should also be perceived and valued when assessing a particular child's developmental status.

SKILL 1.3 Application of Counseling Theories and Techniques to a Specific Situation

Although there are many cases in school settings of students who are in need of emotional counseling and have serious problems in many aspects of their personal life, these problems usually come to the attention of school personnel when the child runs into academic or disruptive classroom behavior. Once a student meets with the counselor, problems of a personal nature may be revealed. Addressing these problems within the context of the goal of success in school may be part of the counselor's role. In the following case, a student has been referred to the counselor because of poor performance. We will then carry it into the counseling situation to better understand what is going on with the student and how resolution was achieved.

In October Donna, a fifteen year old ninth grader, was referred to the school counselor because she was failing her first year algebra course. The teacher did not feel she was capable of doing the work and was suggesting that she drop the course and go into a general math class instead. This would fulfill her math requirement for high school graduation and she would not be behind one year in math. Donna objected to the move. Her parents wanted her to go to college and general math did not meet the requirements for college entrance. Donna had done well in middle school earning grades of 80's and 85's in eighth grade math. Her test scores on diagnostic math tests in May of the previous year when she was in eighth grade, indicated she performed at a 9.3 grade level.

Donna's mother was contacted by telephone and told of the teacher's concern. The mother felt Donna could do the work, that she was lazy and did not apply herself. In discussing with Donna her feelings about why she was failing, the counselor found Donna did not complete her homework assignments because she said when she ran into problems she had no way of solving them. When told she could come in after school for additional help from the teacher Donna said that the days the teacher had designated for extra help were days she had soccer practice.

In discussing a plan for Donna to be successful on the next unit exam in three weeks, it emerged that Donna participated in many non- school activities. She took dance lessons, was out of the house two nights a week for church meetings and to volunteer at the local nursing home reading to elderly patients. She had soccer games on the weekends and her family visited an ailing grandparent on Sundays. Donna had an older sister in her freshman year in college at a school out of town. Her father owned his own business and was active in local politics, and her mother was a teacher.

It was obvious to the counselor that Donna was juggling too many activities and did not have a block of time to devote to her studies. Although she was not failing any of her other courses, her grades were not high enough for entrance into the college that her sister attended and which her parents wanted her to attend. The problem as the counselor saw it was that Donna not only wanted to please her parents by participating in all the out of school activities, but her self esteem and self confidence were derived from these activities. She enjoyed them and did not want to give them up. She continued to think that she could pass the course simply by passing the final exam in June, a school policy.

The counselor decided to use reality therapy with Donna. Donna had a study hall one period a day. She and the counselor decided to use this time for counseling and the teaching of study techniques in the counselor's office. Donna liked this idea as she realized she was not getting any studying done in the study hall because of the disruptive behavior of some of the other students. It was decided Donna and the counselor would talk for twenty minutes and Donna would do her math work for another twenty minutes.
Since Donna did not have the time to see the teacher after school, a student from the honor society would come into the guidance office for twenty minutes every other day to help her study her math. Donna was pleased with this arrangement as the immediate problem of math was being addressed.

In the twenty minutes of counseling time the counselor focused on Donna's lifestyle. Donna had a need to keep busy every minute, the inability to say "no" to many of the projects her parents suggested she do after school, and she had feelings of guilt for her own need to sometimes just do nothing. It was difficult for Donna to accept the fact that she was not able to juggle all these activities, and do well in all of them. She also struggled with the reality that she needed to be able to prioritize and think through what she felt was important in her life, rather than relying on her parents to make these decisions for her. As she began to understand and do better in her algebra class, she continued to feel she could still participate in all her activities.

After Thanksgiving the honor society tutor could no longer help Donna as she needed the time to fill out her own college applications. During the time between Thanksgiving break and Christmas break, Donna's grades in algebra dropped to failing. Donna began to realize even though she could do the math work, as evidenced by her ability to raise her grades when she had the tutor, she could not do it and still maintain her present lifestyle. She needed the discipline to sit down and concentrate. She appealed to the counselor for help in resolving this problem. The counselor began to see a break in Donna's attitude as Donna acknowledged that she needed to change her behavior patterns.

A plan was drawn up for Donna to make time for studying. She decided she would not try out for softball in the spring and would use that time to study and bring her overall grades up. Donna was concerned about telling her parents that she was not going to play softball. A meeting was arranged to present her decision to her parents. At the meeting Donna's parents were surprised and hurt that she had not confided in them. They felt she had been the one who chose to be constantly busy. They did not realize that she felt that her parents demanded the high activity level. The family redefined their goals.

The counselor continued to see Donna throughout the school year. Although Donna and her parents worked at improving her study habits and her priorities, on occasion she slipped, and periodically needed to recommit herself to her original plan. The counselor's support was crucial to Donna's eventual success.

SKILL 1.4 Merits and Limitations of Individual and Group Counseling

Both group and individual counseling require the counselor have knowledge of the theoretical basis of counseling. All major counseling theories can be applied to both situations. During group counseling, the theories take on a more social nature. The theoretical method chosen depends upon the orientation of the counselor, the needs of the client(s), and the goals of the counseling process.

The Scope of the School Counselor's Role

In terms of individual and group counseling, the school counselor's role may vary significantly from one school district to the next. Some districts expect the school counselor to provide ongoing counseling in varied formats as well as crisis intervention and referral. Others limit the work of the counselor to very short term work, focused primarily on the identification of problems with subsequent referral to community resources. Each counselor needs clarity from the head of the department and the school administrators about the scope of his or her work.

With the exception of specialized schools or alternative education programs, most guidance counselors in a school setting are not in a position to provide in-depth mental health counseling. The demands on counselors are many, and the school environment cannot provide the kind of intervention and support some students require. Effective short term counseling with referral for mental health evaluations by qualified personnel in the community often best meets the needs of students. Ongoing therapy should be provided by community agency clinicians or private practitioners in the area. Early identification of substance abuse and mental health concerns followed by collaboration with parent/guardian(s) and appropriate outside referrals can be key functions for school counselors with regard to mental health issues.

Educational and career counseling generally fall within the purview of the school counselor. Other counseling tasks may involve short-term, target-specific psycho-educational groups such as anger management or interpersonal skill development, as well as crisis and/or grief counseling in the event of a death or other trauma in the school community.

Regardless of the extent of a counselor's work in counseling students, there is general agreement that school counselors should not be in the position of school disciplinarian. While there may be an occasion when the school counselor must "write up" a student for a disciplinary problem, as would any faculty or staff member, disciplinary matters should routinely be handled by someone outside of the guidance department. Counselors need to be able to earn and maintain the trust of students; if students don't feel safe with counselors, they are unlikely to seek help from them, or disclose sensitive information to them. Serving as a disciplinarian can undermine trust and interfere with counseling relationships.

Merits of Group Counseling

In a group situation, members have the ability, in a safe and non-threatening atmosphere, to test their attitudes and beliefs against those of the other members of the group. They can receive feedback and discover how they are viewed by others. The group setting can also be a support system for its members, and may be particularly important when members have no other means of emotional support. In this way they can achieve and experiment with some of the goals of becoming emotionally involved without the threat of rejection.

A counseling group is made up of various members of society and thus can be a representation of the client's outer world – the world outside the counseling room. Members can experiment with their styles of interaction with other people in a contained, managed environment. They can then transfer these techniques and behaviors into real life situations. Members of the group can, as they process the observations of the group and their own reactions to others, get a better idea of who they want to become, as well as a better understanding of their own behavior.

For the counselor, the advantages of groups include the ability to reach more clients, to become familiar with differing populations of the school community, and to become more aware of current trends in youth culture.

Limitations of Group Counseling

There may be a tendency to view group counseling as a quick, easy solution when in fact the counselor may find that the work load preparation has increased in proportion to the number of members in the group. Often, individual members need different theoretical approaches as well as extended follow-up.

There is tremendous pressure to accept the group values and substitute them for the previous unworkable value system instead of forming new sets of approaches to the old problem.

Some people function poorly in the group situation. For one reason or another they cannot accept the group's perceptions and fall further into a psychological "funk". Some may find the group setting threatening in spite of the counselor's efforts to create a safe environment.

The personality or acute life circumstances of some individuals may prevent them from making changes in their lives. They may use the group to justify their present status and therefore do not gain from the group's insights.

Individual Counseling

In many school settings, short-term individual counseling is the most common form of intervention. This modality can be utilized spontaneously as problems arise. Further, it is not limited by the scheduling confines of group counseling. The counselor can tailor the interventions to the particular student's needs and make the most of each session. Drawing on varied techniques, the school counselor can respond to immediate situations as well as longer term issues in individual counseling, helping the student effect change in his or her life.

SKILL 1.5   Group Dynamics

Understanding group dynamics is based on knowledge about the psychological and social forces inherent within groups. These forces operate in all human interactions. Over the last fifty years, the concept of group dynamics has become more developed and there exist a number of definitions of group dynamics.

One definition states that group dynamics is a political ideology that is built upon the concept of the organization and management of the group. It emphasizes democratic leadership, equality of membership in decision making and the benefits of group interaction to both society in general and the individual members specifically. Critics of this definition say the emphasis on the group is a method of operating rather than a way of understanding the goals and purpose of the group.

A second definition of group dynamics is derived from the techniques used in group process. Some of these techniques include role-playing, observation and feedback from group members, the decision making process and the concept of "buzz sessions". This type of group process was developed at the National Training Laboratory (www.ntl.org), among other places.

The third definition of group dynamics encompasses the entire field of research and application concerning the nature of groups, the history of their development and their interrelations with individuals, other groups and established institutions. This is the most accepted definition of group dynamics at this time, with a focus on human behavior and relationships.

Some distinctive aspects of the study of group dynamics include:

1. The emphasis on theoretical significance and empirical research.
Originally, functions of group life were debated without the benefit of empirical data. Theories of groups and group dynamics began to be formulated. By the 1920's, scholars began thinking in empirical terms in psychology and sociology.

They became intent on seeking facts based on objective data rather than subjective impressions. They sought data that could be reproduced by other researchers. Consequently, group dynamics research evolved as a phenomenon that could be observed, quantified, measured and experimented. However, such research is highly complex since it involves a number of individuals and many variables, so it is difficult to actually prove many concepts scientifically. Therefore group dynamics research still depends heavily upon theory.

2. Interest in dynamics and interdependence of phenomena.
This refers to the concept that observations of the group depend upon what new phenomena would be created from other conditions yet to be observed. The student of group dynamics hopes to discover general principles about what conditions produce what effects. Many questions have yet to be posed about the interdependence of different conditions upon the dynamics of the group. Some of these complicated questions include the results of change, resistance to change, social pressures, influence, coercion, power and instability. Theories and research of group dynamics attempt to find answers to these types of conditions.

3. Interdisciplinary relevance.
Sociologists, psychologists, cultural anthropologists, political scientists and economists all have an interest in the dynamics of group interaction, as their studies include the behavior of groups. Therefore, general knowledge about the interaction and dynamics of groups touches upon many social science disciplines.

4. Potential application of findings to social practice.
The goal of those studying group dynamics is to help improve the functioning of groups for both societal and individual benefit. Many diverse professions such as labor-management mediation, marriage counseling, and pastoral counseling have much to gain from the scientific study of groups. Supervisors in any profession who have responsibility for other individuals also need this knowledge base. Many training centers have emerged in response to these professionals' need for accurate and effective ways of dealing with groups.

School counselors have many opportunities to utilize knowledge of group dynamics. In the classroom setting, in group counseling, and in understanding the dynamics of peer groups, counselors can draw on understanding the role of the groups that affect individual students' behavior. Always being mindful of the power of groups to affect individuals can be an asset in many school counselor functions.

SKILL 1.6 Communication Skills

Effective communication is essential to the school counselor's ability to do her or his job successfully. The need to listen and respond well cannot be overestimated. Good communication is not only important in order to meet the needs of the students, but also to enhance the functioning of the guidance department and the school's capacity to respond to student needs.

Equally important is the modeling that effective communication provides to students. Good role models are invaluable to students of all ages. When the school counselor shows students how to pay attention to others, express ideas and opinions, make suggestions, and ask questions clearly and respectfully, he or she is teaching skills that students can use throughout their lifetimes.

The essential elements to effective communication are these:

- Listening attentively without interrupting.

- Responding in ways that the speaker knows that she or he has been heard, including direct appreciation and validation of the speaker's views.

- Articulating ideas, opinions, observations and questions clearly and directly.

- Seeking clarification rather than making assumptions about what the other person is saying.

- Maintaining an attitude of respect at all times, including word usage, voice tone, facial expressions and other non-verbal behavior.

- Working to manage one's emotional reactions so they don't interfere with good communication (e.g., not taking other people's comments personally).

Listening and Responding Skills

Listening is a highly subjective and selective activity. Listening is not just hearing words but grasping the meaning the speaker wishes to impart when those words are uttered. The meaning of the words spoken and interpreted depends upon the subjective world of both the speaker and the listener.

Some barriers to good listening are:

1. Hearing what you want to hear, not what is actually said.

2. Not hearing what is said at all due to one's own need to speak. Waiting for the other person to finish so we can speak causes us to think about what we are going to say instead of listening to what is being said

3. We exhibit biased listening when we form an opinion about the value of what is being said and therefore discount the meaning of the words.

4. Emotions, either negative or positive can cause interference with our listening abilities.

5. The presence of both internal and external distractions.

Elements of Good Listening Skills

Effective listening not only involves tuning into the spoken words of the speaker but perceiving the tone of voice, the nonverbal cues given by the speaker and the emphasis given to the words. A good listener is one who consistently, under many circumstances, accurately understands the speaker's meaning by using their listening skills together with their thinking processes.

Lyman Steil developed the SIER Model which includes four stages of listening. These are *sensing,* the attending to a stimulus; *interpreting,* assigning meaning to incoming information; *evaluating* the message by forming a judgment about what is heard; and finally *responding* to the message.

Good listening skills include the following:

1. Create a positive atmosphere by being alert, attentive, and concentrating on the speaker.

2. Make eye contact and maintaining an expression of genuine interest

3. Allow the speaker to finish a thought before responding.

4. Avoid critical judgments in your responses.

5. Make an effort to remember what has been said.

6. Avoid changing the subject unless there is a really good reason to do so. When you must change the subject, explain to the speaker why.

Elements of Good Responding Skills

There are a number of ways one can learn to respond to a speaker to let them know you have heard what he or she is trying to say. If you have listened well and thoughtfully to what the person is saying, your response will be appropriate, you will give good feedback and the speaker will feel good about the fact that you have heard what was said.

Good responding skills include:

1. Clarify the meaning of what was said by checking assumptions you have made as the listener to be sure you understand.

2. Continue to maintain eye contact as you give feedback.

3. Keep anger and other emotions out of the interaction. Try to express your feelings in a non-threatening way.

4. Help the other person in problem solving by responding positively and asking good questions.

5. Directly express your appreciation of the speaker's ideas, even if you disagree with them. You can address disagreements more effectively once you have thanked the speaker for sharing his/her ideas.

6. Be physically alert and use appropriate body language.

7. Reflect the person's feelings back to them.

8. Summarize the major ideas and concepts for further clarifications.

9. Use verbal and nonverbal reinforcers (such as head nods) to let the speaker know his/her message has been received.

10. Maintain a comfortable social distance.

11. Give constructive feedback: this is feedback that is descriptive not evaluative, offered not imposed, and focused on behavior rather than personal characteristics. Pay attention to the timing of feedback as well.

These websites offer useful tips on listening and responding skills:
www.taft.cc.ca.us/lrc/class/assignments/actlisten.html,
crs.uvm.edu/gopher/nerl/personal/comm/e.html,
www.nasua.org/informationandreferral/TipSheet1ActiveListening.pdf , and
www.psu.edu/dus/cfe/actvlstn.htm.

SKILL 1.7   Stressors Affecting Students and School Performance

Students' academic performance and behavior is impacted not only by the school environment but also by a range of external factors. Stressors can negatively impact academic achievement by making it difficult for the student to focus on learning. When a student is homeless, for example, it may be difficult for him or her to attend in class because of lack of sleep, worry about what is happening with a parent, concerns about where dinner is coming from and other pressing life issues. Similarly, if a child is being abused at home, he or she may have difficulties with attention and focus.

Some stressors, such as medical conditions, may prevent a child from participating in some school activities or require homebound instruction. While accommodations need to be made for alternative programming, the inability to be "part of the group" still may impair peer relationships and affect skill development and motivation.

Stressors can also have a less direct impact. A challenging home life may make it hard for a student to complete homework assignments or study effectively. Chronic stress and traumatic events also contribute to a lack of self confidence, poor motivation, inadequate social skills, depression, anxiety, and other mental health problems. These difficulties may interfere with a student's ability to participate effectively in the school environment. They can also disrupt the student's efforts to study and do homework.

Individuals respond in different ways to the same or similar stressors, and the impact of such stressors needs to be assessed for each student. Mitigating factors include coping skills, personality traits, prior experience with stress and trauma, the degree of social isolation created by the stressful event(s), the quality of attachment to and presence of significant adults in the student's life, and the amount and kind of support the student receives in relation to the stressor.

Special Populations

Although every student has special needs because he or she is an individual, there are some students who, by virtue of birth or life circumstance, belong to a group with specific needs. Again, as noted previously, not all children and adolescents who belong to a certain group will necessarily fit a description or profile of group characteristics, because each student is an individual. For example, a particular girl may express a learning style more commonly associated with boys.

However, for the purpose of alerting school counselors to issues their students may face, some factors that may be of concern to selected populations are noted below.

Migrant worker families:

- Chronic disruption in living circumstances and education, resulting in significant gaps in learning.
- Social isolation.
- Inadequate nutrition and medical care.
- Bias due to stereotyping.
- Stress due to the problems noted above as well as economic hardship.

Immigrant families and those for whom English is a second language:

- Loss of homeland and extended family.
- Difficulties with learning, socialization and peer group acceptance due to language limitations.
- Bias due to stereotyping.
- Post-traumatic stress due to precipitating events that prompted immigration and/or losses associated with relocation.

Homeless families:

- Multiple losses and traumas, and related post-traumatic stress.
- Disruption in living circumstances and education, resulting in significant gaps in learning.
- Inadequate nutrition, sleep and medical care.
- Underlying anxiety due to chaotic and/or unpredictable environment.
- Absenteeism for various reasons.

Families displaced due to catastrophic events (such as hurricanes):

- Multiple losses and traumas, and related post-traumatic stress.
- Disruption in living circumstances and education.

- Lack of social network and extended family support.
- Sudden change in economic circumstances.

Families living in poverty:

- Chronic stress due to economic hardship and challenging life circumstances.
- Inadequate resources for special events at school (field trips, testing, dances, sporting events, etc.).
- Inadequate nutrition and medical care.
- Absenteeism due to the need to attend to pressing family matters.

Gifted and talented students:

- Boredom, which may lead to behavior problems.
- Need for special services and/or creative programming.
- Bias due to stereotyping.

Learning support and special education students:

- Increased need for appropriate attention and support from faculty and staff.
- Need for evaluation, special services and/or creative programming.
- Bias due to stereotyping.

Emotional support students:

- Presence of significant mental health issues.
- Increased need for appropriate attention from faculty and staff, including consultation with other professionals, evaluation, referral, and follow-up.
- Need for special services.

Child Abuse and Neglect

Governmental and nongovernmental sources report that between 12 and 15 children out of every thousand children are abused each year by immediate family members or people living in the home. This does not include abuse and violence perpetrated by others outside the home. Also, these numbers reflect only reported cases of abuse. Abuse or neglect may occur for years before it is investigated; in other cases, abuse continues unchecked. Many children are fearful about reporting abuse for a range of reasons, including the desire to protect one's caregivers and worry about the consequences of reporting.

Given the prevalence of abuse and neglect, it is important the counselor recognizes potential signs of child abuse and neglect. When behavioral indicators are present, counselors should meet with students individually to gather more information about suspected abuse, and to determine who in the child's family or network can be an ally.

The easiest type of abuse to detect is physical abuse. There are unexplained bruises, bite marks, burns, fractures and other physical indicators that a child has been physically abused. In addition the child can exhibit withdrawal and aggressive behavior, self-destructive behavior, self-injury (such as sticking a pencil into parts of the body or pinching oneself), and avoidance of physical contact with others.

Child neglect is indicated by the need for medical attention, reported lack of supervision, dirty unkempt and generally poor hygiene, as well as always being hungry. Common behavioral manifestations are falling asleep inappropriately, stealing food, frequent absences, expressions of hunger and self-destructive behaviors.

For the child who has been sexually abused there may be some difficulty in sitting or walking, stained clothing, venereal disease and pain or itching in the genital area. The behavioral manifestations can be quite varied. Overtly sexualized behavior in children under the age of 12 may be an indicator, as can attention problems in school work, self-injury, depression, extremely volatile emotions, suicidal thoughts or gestures, and an inability to control one's behavior in children of all ages.

For the emotionally abused child the indicators are eating disorders, sleeping problems, loss of energy and chronic complaints. The behavior manifestations include depression, low self-esteem, lack of self confidence, poor peer relations, and suicidal thoughts or gestures.

The Center for Disease Control has information about child abuse and neglect at www.cdc.gov/ncipc/dvp/CMP/default.htm. Information about child sexual abuse is also available at www.nlm.nih.gov/medlineplus/childsexualabuse.html.

Bullying, Stereotyping and Prejudice

Increasing, schools are finding they need to take action to address stereotyping, prejudice and bullying among students. A number of factors lead to bullying behavior. Stereotypes and prejudice are major contributors, along with personal characteristics and life experiences of the bullying student.

Certain characteristics and personality traits of other individuals may be targeted for prejudice and stereotyping. Some of these are based on students who belong to a specific class such as gender, race, ethnicity, religion, physical ability, sexual orientation, and age. Stereotypes abound in our culture regarding these characteristics, and these stereotypes are frequently brought into the school setting and used as the basis for teasing and bullying.

However, such stereotypes are not the only source of bias. Anything that makes a person different in the eyes of the perceiver – anything out of the "norm" – can trigger ridicule, ostracism, hate and violence. Some of these are:

- attractiveness vs. unattractiveness
- thin vs. obese individuals
- effeminate males vs. virile males
- masculine females vs. feminine females
- "in" group vs. "out" group (i.e., cool vs. not-cool)

The presence of difference, in and of itself, is not a problem in the larger world or the school setting. In fact, in a positive school environment, such differences are acknowledged and appreciated. The important issue, however, is the way individuals who are perceived as different are treated, and how that treatment affects the social and emotional well-being of the targeted individuals.

There is evidence to suggest that the self-esteem of a student is directly affected by this type of stereotyping. The stereotyping and its effects can begin as early as the first time a child enters school and may continue throughout the life span. The accuracy of the impressions are not relevant as the person targeted soon "fulfills the prophecy" or begins to have emotional problems due to the trauma resulting from prejudice and bullying.

The targeted individual often displays the following:

1. Believes there is something wrong with them and considers him/herself a "loser."
2. Develops emotional problems connected with the perceived inferiority.
3. Manifests a lack of motivation and desire to excel as "It doesn't matter what I do as I never do anything right."
4. Displays personality problems.
5. Begins to feel life isn't worth living and contemplates suicide.
6. Begins to harbor thoughts of violence against the perpetrators of the perceived insult.
7. In extreme cases, carries out an act of self-violence or violence against others.

If not educated to accept differences among people, the perpetrator of the stereotyping, prejudice or other bullying type activities is likely to:

1. Escalate the activity.
2. Enlist others to engage in the activity.
3. Become firm in their beliefs that the targeted individual is undesirable.
4. Feel superior to the targeted individual or groups and justify his/her actions.
5. Become resistant to changing attitudes and incorporate them into a way of life.
6. Resort to violence after justifying the violence in his/her mind.

Programs to combat stereotyping, prejudice and biases should be part of the school curriculum. Although the labeling of entire groups of people is irrational, the school must respond rationally and create programs to deal with these issues. Students can be taught to respect the rights of others by programs of cooperation and conflict resolution.

A good website for students as well as teachers and counselors on bullying prevention can be found at **stopbullyingnow.hrsa.gov/index.asp**.

Aggression, Violence, Conflict Resolution and Interpersonal Relations

In 2005, the federal Centers for Disease Control and Prevention did a national survey of high school students' risk behaviors and reported this information in relation to school violence:

• 13.6% reported being in a physical fight on school property in the 12 months preceding the survey.

• 18.2% of male students and 8.8% of female students reported being in a physical fight on school property in the 12 months preceding the survey.

• 29.8% of students reported having property stolen or deliberately damaged on school property.

• 6.0% did not go to school on one or more days in the 30 days preceding the survey because they felt unsafe at school or on their way to or from school.

• 6.5% reported carrying a weapon (gun, knife or club) on school property on one or more days in the 30 days preceding the survey.

• 7.9% reported being threatened or injured with a weapon on school property one or more times in the 12 months preceding the survey."

(Source: www.cdc.gov/ncipc/dvp/YV_DataSheet.pdf)

We are all familiar with the school shootings that occur once in a while. However, the above data reflect the equally troubling and perhaps more relevant facts regarding everyday violence in schools. A major factor contributing to violence in schools is the acceptance of violence as a "normal" reaction to perceived injustices. Media depictions of violence may convey a perception that violent retaliation is "normal" and common. Easy access to guns and other weapons, and the effect of both drug abuse and the way the drug culture permeates the larger culture also may contribute to school violence.

In the school setting, administrators, teachers, counselors and support staff have has the responsibility to make the school a safe place for all students. Their goal should be to maximize the potential for learning, emphasize the benefits of education, and to create an environment where teachers can educate all students, even disruptive ones.

Clear policies that delineate safety and guide behavior are useful. Policies should exist articulating appropriate behavior on school property and at school events with regard to the following topics, as well as others:

1. Weapons
2. Homicidal and/or suicidal intent
3. Use of drugs and alcohol
4. Self-harm
5. Sexual harassment
6. Bullying
7. Violent threats

However, policies are not enough. Preventing violence and resolving conflicts in interpersonal relations are fundamentally related. Programs of violence prevention must be accompanied by programs of constructive conflict resolution so student can learn methods of positive interactions with others, including those who are different. Not only do these programs help create a safe environment in the schools, but they also teach students the skills to resolve future conflicts in their careers, family, and community as adults. A program of violence prevention and conflict resolution acknowledges that while destructive and violent conflicts may be out of control in our society we can strive to minimize them in any particular school, home or other setting.

The conflict resolution program should:
1. Create an atmosphere of cooperation.
2. Have a component of peer meditation training that teaches negotiation, mediation and arbitration skills to students and teachers.
3. Include units in academic classes on methods of negotiation, mediation and arbitration.

Active violence prevention programs include:

1. The elimination of weapons in school by metal detectors, random locker searches and appropriate personnel to monitor the open school areas.
2. A law enforcement presence on the surrounding property of the school for monitoring and enforcement purposes.
3. Training programs for faculty and staff so they are better able to recognize and intervene before and during violent confrontations.
4. A system for identifying students who are or are at risking of becoming perpetrators of violence and refer them to behavior modification, anger management or other appropriate programs.
5. The creation of a district task force to identify and address the causes of violence in the school district.
6. Effective policies addressing violent behavior and a program that assures student protection if they feel they are in danger.
7. Counseling and/or referral for students traumatized by violence.

Bullying and violence prevention resources are available at **www.cdc.gov/ncipc/dvp/YVP/YVP-data.htm** and **mentalhealth.samhsa.gov/15plus/aboutbullying.asp**.

The National Youth Violence Prevention Resource Center offers resources not only on bullying and violence prevention but also addresses substance abuse and other safety issues for teens at www.safeyouth.org/scripts/topics/school.asp.

Substance Abuse and Addiction

Although solving problems of addiction and substance abuse is a long term counseling activity it is, unfortunately, not a feasible activity for the school counselor due to other duties the counselor is expected to perform, the number of students for which the counselor is responsible, and the lack of time in the school day to do an adequate job of intervention. There may be situations where student s needs residential care to combat the addiction and substance abuse that can only be provided by a health related agency.

The job of the school counselor is to recognize the signs of addiction and substance abuse and, with the cooperation of the student's parents, make referrals to the proper agency for treatment. It is also the counselor's job to, follow-up with the chosen agency about the progress of the student, and provide for the transition of the student back into the school setting. Some of the indicators of substance abuse are:

1. Recurrent use resulting in an inability to perform at school and home.
2. Continued use in dangerous situations despite the possibility of physical harm, such as driving a motor vehicle or swimming while under the influence.

3. Continued use that results in legal problems such as prosecution for drunken driving, arrests for disturbing the peace and possession of a controlled substance.
4. Inability to stop using the controlled substance in spite of social problems such as fights, conflict with family and peers, and poor school performance.

The element of denial is often involved when confronting a student with a substance abuse problem. It may be effective for the school to require the student alcohol and/or drug counseling before returning to school if there has been a breach of school rules and policies by the student. A referral to a professional in the drug abuse field for an evaluation is always an appropriate action when counselors are concerned about the possibility of addiction.

Suicide, Self-Injury, Eating Disorders and Interpersonal Violence

The problems of suicide, anorexia, bulimia, sexual assault, dating violence and self-injury are serious, often long term counseling problems beyond the scope of a school counselor's duties. They may require that the counselor communicate with a range of community agencies and personnel. The school counselor's primary tasks are identification, crisis counseling, parental notification, referral, support, and follow up. It is essential that the counselor utilize the school's protocol in these instances, and report the information to school administration. It may also be appropriate for the school counselor to involve the student assistance team within the school setting.

The American Psychiatric Association notes on their webpage for **teen suicide** that although "...the teen suicide rate has declined by over 25 percent since the early 1990s, suicide is the third leading cause of death among young people ages 15 to 24." (See www.healthyminds.org/multimedia/teensuicide.pdf.)

They go on to detail the following statistics about teen suicide:
- It is estimated that depression increases the risk of a first suicide attempt by at least 14-fold.
- Over half of all kids who suffer from depression will eventually attempt suicide at least once, and more than seven percent will die as a result.
- Four times as many men commit suicide than women, but young women attempt suicide three times more frequently than young men.
- Fifty-three percent of young people who commit suicide abuse substances.
- Firearms are used in a little more than half of all youth suicides."

One of the most common and effective methods school personnel have to recognize the suicidal student is in the writings of that student. Often, an English teacher will come to the counselor with a sample of a student's writing that suggests thoughts and/or plans of suicide. Other times, the counselor may learn that the student is thinking about suicide by comments made directly by the student, or from friends of the student who are concerned.

When such information comes to the attention of the counselor, the counselor should meet as soon as possible with the student. If the student is known to the counselor and a rapport has been built, it is appropriate to speak directly with the student, with the teacher's permission, about the material of concern. Even if the counselor does not already have a relationship with the student, sometimes the counselor must proceed without a prior connection and work at building rapport in the moment.

If confirmation of the suicidal intent is received from the student (and in many cases, even if the student does not confirm suicidal intent), the counselor has a duty to inform the parent/guardian(s), the school administration and the school nurse, that the student is currently at risk. Plans for intervention should be made at the time of this discovery. Do not delay until the next day, or until after a weekend. Once the parent/guardian(s) and/or appropriate professionals are notified, the treatment is in the hands of those who have the skills and authority to deal with the problem.

Self-injury is not uncommon in adolescents and sometimes occurs in middle school students as well. Self-injury is direct harm to the body, such as cutting or burning; it is distinguished from a suicide attempt in that the intent behind the self-injury is *not* connected to a wish to die. Self-injury serves to release tension and help the student manage emotional pain and distress. The counselor may learn about such behavior by direct observation (scars, wounds, bandages) or from the student engaging in self-injury or their friends. Like eating disorders, addressing this issue is a long term problem and requires referral to appropriate mental health professionals. However, school counselors may be in the position of providing support to teen who self-injure as well as offering information and referral.

For more information about self-injury, go to www.healingselfinjury.org/.

Anorexia nervosa, where someone starves him / herself, or its variant, **bulimia**, where the person alternately binges on food and then purges by vomiting or using laxatives, are eating disorders that also arise particularly in adolescence. Again, the counselor may recognize the problem by direct observation and/or reports from the student's friends and peers. Addressing these problems with students can be difficult because the student often truly believes he/she is overweight, or has normal eating patterns.

Eating disorders are often associated with depression and low self-esteem, and, unchecked, can lead to malnutrition, body chemistry imbalance, cessation of the menstrual cycle and other endocrine dysfunctions.

See kidshealth.org/parent/nutrition_fit/nutrition/eating_disorders.html for more information, warning signs, and resources for coping with eating disorders in teens.

When a counselor learns that a student may have an eating disorder, is self-injuring, or is thought to be at risk for suicide, s/he needs to meet with the student to explore the student's perceptions and concerns. It is also the professional responsibility of the counselor along with the school nurse and other medical school personnel, to inform the parent/guardian(s). The parent/guardian(s) need to be aware of the problem and may also need information, support and encouragement in seeking help for their child from the appropriate medical or mental health professional. The school's student assistance team might also be useful in aiding with referral, support, and follow up.

Interpersonal violence is another common problem among teens. One in three teenagers experiences dating violence (www.acadv.org/dating.html) and a number of teens are also raped or sexually assaulted by either an acquaintance or stranger. The issue of interpersonal physical or sexual violence is likely to be brought to school counselors along with the psychological issues noted above. Such situations require the same sensitivity and attention that other serious issues demand, including contact with parent/guardian(s) and appropriate referrals. These cases may also require the involvement of law enforcement personnel.

SKILL 1.8 Guidance Activities

Many guidance functions are achieved through the context of individual counseling or specific group counseling sessions. School counselors also engage in a range of guidance activities and specialized programs, and in the various ways they communicate with students (addressed in the next section). Appraisal, consultation, research, program evaluation and career development are explored in more depth elsewhere in this guide. However, some of the activities that counselors might be involved in are detailed below.

Student Skill Development

When students succeed in their studies they are eager to continue their education. They are more likely, too, to understand the relationship between the acquisition of education and their future lifestyles. When students do not succeed it is very difficult for them to see the value of education and how it relates to their future. When basic survival is demanding the student's attention, and the student does poorly in school, and the tendency to drop out of school or to engage in illicit profitable activities, such as crime and drug dealing, has a fatal attraction.

Counselors can help students facing these challenges to marshal resources to cope with life, as well as help them learn to defer present wants and needs (and peer pressure) in order to receive enhanced rewards at a later date. Further, these students may need specific support regarding academic achievement such as tutoring or special classes.

Exposure to role models who have escaped from poverty and/or crime is important for some students. Persuading such role models to mentor unmotivated students, and providing satisfying educational opportunities in the school may help students explore their potential more fully. Innovative programs can be found by using the resources of the community, the cooperation of parents and the resources of the school. There is also the availability of grant monies to implement programs for unmotivated students in some settings.

Helping students develop skills in various arenas can also be central to school and subsequent career success. Three important skill areas are delineated here: decision-making, studying, and employability.

Helping Students with Decision Making

For adolescents, decision making can be an overwhelming task. Adolescence is a time of self-definition, and therefore many teenagers are faced with both real and imagined crucial life decisions. They may ask "What if I make the wrong decision and I cannot change the course of my life?"

The school counselor's role is to help students understand the decision making process. This can help the student minimize the impact of any one decision causing irreversible harm to the student's present or future. An example of the need for good decision making skills is evident with regard to post-secondary education: a senior has received multiple offers from colleges and cannot decide on which offer to accept.

The process of decision-making can be broken down into the following steps:

1. Define the problem clearly.
2. Formulate goals of ideal, acceptable and unacceptable outcomes.

3. Delineate all the possible options, including the option of making no decision at all.
4. Explore the barriers to all the options.
5. Explore the consequences of eliminating one or more of the options.
6. Narrow the options down to manageable choices.
7. Make an informed decision based upon the manageable choices.

Elementary and middle school counselors may not face the same demands regarding student decision-making. However, helping students with decisions regarding elective courses and extracurricular activities, for example, can facilitate better decision making at the high school level.

Teaching Study Skills

Efficient ways of studying have been researched for years by psychologists. Research has yielded a method of studying that helps students retain information and learn in a more organized manner. The following suggestions are the result of these experiments.

1. Make a schedule and stick to it. Study at a certain time each day.

2. Find a place that is comfortable, suits your individual learning style, and is consistently available and convenient.

3. Have all the materials needed in one place before starting work so study will not be interrupted.

4. Study every day in order to develop the habit of knowing how to study when it is really needed.

5. Keep an accurate and comprehensible notebook in case you need to refer to it.

6. Keep a careful record of assignments. Use a calendar for due dates of all projects.
7. Use short cut devices for retaining information such as flash cards, self-tests or "cover cards" which succinctly detail the material to be retained. Repeat the material orally.

8. Take good notes that list the main points of the material.

9. After learning the material, continue to study to "over-learn." This helps retain the material for a longer period of time.

10. Review frequently after learning the material for the first time.

Assisting Students to Develop Employability Skills

Throughout a student's high school career the opportunity to relate subject matter to career and job opportunities should be included in the curriculum of each subject. Job fairs and other types of exposure to job requirements should be presented to students at every opportunity.

An additional method of motivating students to acquire employable skills is to engage community businesses in making a commitment to employ students who adequately prepare themselves for entrance into the job market of the sponsoring business or industry. Apprenticeships, internships and supervised employment while still in school, as a requirement for graduation in a particular area, will encourage students to acquire the skills needed to go from high school graduation to a job that is waiting for them.

When students have incentives they are more likely to work at acquiring the math, English, science and technical skills required by the employer. They will also work at studying other subject areas in which they are not as interested in order to obtain the requirements needed for graduation. When they are working in satisfying positions, they can then have a concrete opportunity to see the need for future education; they may also be able to get their tuition paid for by their employer.

Developing Special Programs to Meet Identified Needs

Although many of the school counselor's tasks are designated by the overall plan of the guidance program, there is occasionally the need to develop special programs to cope with an emerging problem or respond to a particular group of students. Such a need may be identified by a formal needs assessment or, more commonly, by a classroom management problem, teacher observations or direct knowledge of the counselor. A specific program to address the need can be a creative solution and serve to prevent an escalation of the problem.

Two examples of special programs are the Lunch Bunch and an anger management mini-group. The Lunch Bunch is an opportunity for new students to meet with other students new to the district and the counselor in a small group at lunch time. Meeting in a somewhat informal setting while eating lunch can be useful and non-threatening for new students. It addresses the discomfort some students feel at lunch time when long-time friends sit together. It helps build peer relationships as well as a connection with the school counselor. It can, after a few meetings, include "old" students to help the students build bridges into the larger school community. The Lunch Bunch should only meet short-term (4-6 times) once a week at the same time, in order to facilitate this process of integration.

A psycho-educational group focused on anger management can be an opportunity for violence and bullying prevention as well as an intervention strategy. In this setting (which is more formal than the Lunch Bunch, for example) the school counselor meets with a small group (6-8) of students who need help with anger management skills. They can be self-selected or identified by the counselor, teachers and other staff. In this group, skills are taught and information shared. Behavior modification approaches may also be employed. Further, students can discuss their concerns about and struggles with anger and other emotions.

Ideally, the school counselor has students complete evaluation forms following their involvement in such special programs, in order to assess their effectiveness. This information could be used in deciding to offer the program again, modifying the program or developing new programs. Other staff members and teachers who are involved in the program or are able to observe the effects of the program may also be solicited for their feedback.

SKILL 1.9   Communicating Information to Students

The major task of the counselor in the school is communication: communication with the student, the parent/guardian, teachers, school administrators and support staff members, other professionals, people in the community and sometimes even members of the media. The primary client is the student.

The ability to create rapport and meaningful relationships with students and others is the sign of an effective counselor. When the counselor has the trust of the student, the student is much more likely to listen to and act on the counselor's suggestions. Keeping information confidential, within the confines of the need for parental notification and other school policies, is essential to building trust.

If the counselor does not keep information confidential, trust is destroyed, and it is harder to help the student grow and mature. Trust is built up gradually. In order to facilitate trust, information given to the student must always be true, accurate and timely. The counselor must be a visible presence in the school, and be available to students. There are many ways to make contact with students, both formally and informally. When such an atmosphere of accessibility is created, students will be much more inclined to contact the counselor in time of need and crisis.

A. Newsletters

Monthly newsletters to a student's home inform the student and the parent/guardian about what is happening in the world of guidance. Newsletters should contain deadline dates for national exams, dates of specific college visitations, notice of aptitude and school generated exams, scholarship deadlines, workshops about financial, and other items of interest that are occurring in the Guidance Department and the community at large. It may feature some of the guidance clerical staff and their duties, procedures for making appointments with the staff and any other information that would facilitate connection and communication. If the principal or other school administrator sends out a monthly bulletin, a section of that newsletter could be set aside for guidance news.

B. Homeroom and Classroom Visitations

Visiting homerooms is an efficient way for counselors to get to know students, . Students are also able to ask questions or be reminded of issues they may wish to discuss with the counselor. It is helpful for students to see guidance counselors in various settings throughout the school so they don't associate the counselor only with problems or trouble.

Visiting the classroom is also a means of disseminating information directly to students. For example, when it comes time to schedule the high school student for the following year, the homeroom visiting the homeroom (or other classes such as social sciences) creates an opportunity to share the course schedule and other information efficiently..

C. Individual Interviews

Much of the real work of counseling occurs in the individual interviews the counselor holds with the student. These interviews should occur on a regular basis. It is often quite difficult to schedule all students for individual interviews but it is important that this be done. At the high school level, freshmen and seniors should be scheduled as soon as possible within the first month of school. The freshmen, in order to get acquainted and find out if there are any adjustment problems, and the seniors to inform them about post-secondary training and college application deadlines, tests needed for entrance to college, and other plans for post high school activities. The initial interviews with freshmen can also help create the basis of trust needed to help students with future problems.

TEACHER CERTIFICATION STUDY GUIDE

D. Dissemination of Forms

Each school has systematic ways to distribute necessary information to students. This might include applications for national exams, local and state scholarships, as well as other guidance-related material. Some schools utilize the homeroom setting; others send home this information to individual students or give it out in individual interviews. Quite often the counselor has access to a large group of students during a study hall period or in the cafeteria. A study hall situation may offer an ideal chance for answering questions about testing and other issues students wish to discuss.

E. Intercom Announcements

Announcements over the school intercom system are an excellent vehicle to remind students of guidance and other activities that are occurring on a specific day. It is also a means of informing students of upcoming activities and deadline dates.

F. Informal Chance Meetings

It is important that the counselor get out of the office some time during the school day to meet students in areas they frequent during their school time. The cafeteria, the hallways, and the student lounge are all places the counselor can meet students, ask how they are doing, remind them of specific issues and make appointments for meetings.

SKILL 1.10 Resources and Evaluation Materials for Counseling Activities

A. Current Journals

The counselor should belong to professional organizations such as the local and state branches of the American Counseling Association, teacher organizations that relate to their work in developmental areas such as reading and special education, and other broad education organizations such as Phi Delta Kappa. The journals that are published by these organizations have a wealth of information about current trends, theories and practices in the field.

B. Commercial Advertising

Students and parents are bombarded with commercial advertising that often involve education programs. It is important that the counselor is aware of these programs and evaluates them. Many times students look to the counselor to determine the legitimacy of these offers. Advertisements for scholarship searches, tutoring services and computer programs for improvement of grades are some of the ways advertisers entice parents and students to buy their products.

C. Publishing Houses

Once the counselor is registered as a licensed professional, he/she will receive solicitations for new publications, new programs and memberships in related organizations. While there is a tendency to toss all this information into the trash, some of it is valuable and should at least be perused. A system can be devised among counseling staff for each counselor to be responsible for specific areas and to share this pertinent material at staff meetings.

D. College Visitations

In order to keep up with new programs colleges are offering to students and to become familiar with the admissions staff at the different institutions, it is important for the counselor to visit these schools, and, at least once a year, take an out of area visit to schools in which some of their students have taken an interest. Quite often students are unable to visit a school before applying and the counselor visitation can help a particular student by providing information about the characteristics of that school. The armed forces offer trips to military installations to familiarize the counselor with the educational programs of the particular branch of the service represented. These are usually free or low cost. The school district may be persuaded to provide funds from the guidance budget for some of these visitations.

E. College Night

A joint college night sponsored by all the schools in the county can be both a service to the students and a possible fund raiser. If the colleges are charged a small fee for presenting and if a dinner is provided, the counselors can raise money for scholarships for needy and deserving students. It is also good public relations for the department when they can present a scholarship to a student at the awards night program.

F. Visitation to Other School Programs

Counselors can learn from innovative programs instituted by other schools by visiting these programs and evaluating their good and bad aspects. After a program has been in practice for a period of time, the originators of the program are aware of improvements that should be made. If your school is interested in starting the program, it can be beneficial to learn from the mistakes of others and to be able to offer an improved version of the program.

G. Workshops and Conventions

Workshops and conventions are a valuable resource for new ideas and innovative practices. They are also a vehicle for learning new state and federal rules and regulations. When a counselor belongs to professional organizations, information about coming events is mailed to the counselor well in advance of the event. The counselor can then choose the event they wish to attend depending on interest and expertise. In addition, counselors who have expertise in a particular area can present at these programs. This gives the counselor the chance to share their ideas with others and also lends a degree of prestige to the school in which they are employed. Local opportunities should not be excluded; nearby colleges or agencies may offer relevant continuing education programs as well as the chance to network with potential referrals.

COMPETENCY 1.0   SUMMARY

Psychoanalysis, (Sigmund Freud) Unconscious motivation. Oral, anal, phallic, latency, and genital stages of development.

Adlerian (Alfred Adler): Consciousness. Capacity to reach optimal functioning. Experiences are not as important as our attitudes about our experiences. Inferiority. Lifestyle assessment and basic mistakes.

Behavior Therapy (B.F. Skinner): Learned behavior. Goal of therapy is to eliminate negative learned behaviors and replace them with positive ones through a process of conditioning and reinforcement.

Cognitive-Behavior Therapy: Change negative behavior by changing false thinking and feelings. (Albert Ellis)—Rational Emotive Therapy (RET): action and practice can combat irrational thoughts and beliefs.

Existential Therapy: (Rollo May, Victor Frankl) Loneliness, isolation, alienation, meaninglessness, freedom, and death. We are free and therefore responsible for our actions and the results of those actions and choices.

Person-Centered Therapy: (Carl Rogers) Nondirective. Clients have the ability to determine how to self-actualize. Trust is essential for this ability to develop. Active listening and reflecting. The counselor-client relationship is all-important.

Gestalt: (Frederick Perls) Stresses the "here and now." Unfinished business from the past prevents the individual from adequately functioning in the present.

Reality Therapy: (William Glasser) Emphasizes individual responsibility, personal accountability, the use of goal-setting, and contracts. Popular in schools because of its short-term focus.

Solution-Focused Therapy: (Steve deShazer and Insoo Kim Berg) Quick and effective therapy that focuses on implementing a picture of how the client will act after solving a problem.

Important Counselor Skills: Active Listening, Reflection, Empathy.

The Decision-Making Process can be used to help students make choices:

1. Define the problem.
2. State desired outcomes.
3. Explore the possible options, (including the option of making no decision at all.)
4. Explore the barriers to all the options.
5. Explore the consequences of eliminating one or more of the options.
6. Narrow the options down to manageable choices.
7. Make an informed decision based upon the choices.

Counselors must participate in the creation of appropriate school programming, such as those which address stereotyping, stress, sexual harassment, conflict resolution, violence prevention, and substance abuse prevention. Further, working toward a **positive school environment** is critical for prevention of problems and student success.

Counselors must be **alert to the signs of students in need of referral** to more specialized community mental health services, including students with substance abuse issues or addiction, eating disorders, depression, the capacity for violence, or the potential for suicide.

In the case of students at risk of harming themselves or of harming others, the counselor must **notify appropriate officials**, parent/guardian(s) and warn individuals who may be in danger.

Counselors should maintain **regular communication** with students, parents, and the surrounding community. This can be accomplished through the use of newsletters or bulletins, newspaper announcements, and well-maintained websites. Topics should cover test administration dates, scheduling deadlines, parent nights, and school-sponsored events.

Counselors should meet with students individually as often as their schedules allow, but may also visit classrooms to meet with student groups. The guidance counselors also often have responsibility for coordinating "college nights" and "job fairs." Parents and students will look to the counselor to provide accurate information concerning college applications, scholarships, and financial aid applications.

COMPETENCY 2.0　KNOWLEDGE OF STUDENT APPRAISAL

Aside from school psychologists, counselors are the school professionals most likely to be called upon to interpret assessment results for students, parents, teachers, and administrators. For this reason, counselors must possess a thorough understanding of the concepts and terminology associated with tests and measurement.

Skill 2.1　Knowledge of Measurement Concepts

The language of testing is unique, and knowledge of interpretation of test data is an important part of the appraisal procedure. Some common terms used in testing and measurement are:

Correlation coefficient - a statistical concept in test validity that measures the relationship between two factors.

Derived score - any score that is not a raw score. It is obtained from a formula that uses the raw score data.

Norming - the scores obtained by a randomly selected group of test takers for the purpose of comparison to future groups of test takers to determine uniform levels of success on the tested information.

Raw Score - the basic score that is usually obtained by counting the number of answers right. It can also be obtained by using the number of answers wrong. The authors of the test can determine any other way to define a raw score. The way the score is defined is noted in the test manual.

Reliability - how dependable or consistent the test is. The three types of reliability are: 1) **scorer reliability:** how consistently different scorers arrive at the same score; often used as a measurement when grading essays or subjective tests; 2) **content reliability**: the degree to which all questions measure the content; 3) **temporal reliability**: how dependable the test is over a long period of time.

Reliability coefficient - a statistical concept in test validity that measures how reliable the relationship is between two factors.

Standard deviation - the specific interval between bands of scores; each interval indicates a different level of achievement.

Standard error of measurement - the inaccuracy of a test caused by chance. Every test has some element of inaccuracy or unreliability so this element of the test is taken into consideration when evaluating the test results. The degree of error is reported in the use of the term standard deviation, which is a band of scores. The formula is this: the square root of 1 minus the reliability coefficient, thus obtaining the standard error of measurement.

Standard score - an indication of the distance between the raw score and the mean of the norm in terms of the standard deviation.

Standardization - Researchers, other than the authors of the test, have provided the protocol to be used to administer the exam, including the provision that the test will be given and scored in the same way at each administration.

Stanine - an interpretation of placement often used in achievement tests. It is a measurement that runs from 1 to 9 and is a band of about one-half a standard deviation in width. Scores are based on percentile values.

Usability - the consideration given to cost, ease of administration, and time taken to score in the administration of the test.

Validity - This is the concept of "does the test, test what it is supposed to test?" In other words, how meaningful is the test? There are four types of validity:

1. **face validity**: Does it look like it may test what it should? (This is not a very dependable source of information.)
2. **content validity**: Is there a close connection between what is taught and what is being tested?
3. **construct validity**: What is the statistical relationship between the scores and another variable that should relate to the test?
4. **empirical validity**: What is the correlation coefficient between the scores and some standard of performance?

SKILL 2.2 Conditions Affecting Test Results

Testing Room Environment - The comfort of the room and the desk or table and chairs can affect the outcome of the test. The room should be well lighted and ventilated, free of noise and extraneous sound. A minimum distance should be maintained between desks, alternating seats if possible, and the students should be able to hear the directions clearly. The desk should be large enough to provide enough writing space for both the test and the answer sheet

Physical and Mental Condition of the Test Taker - The scores obtained on any test depend to a certain extend on the student's physical and mental condition. Tests should never be scheduled to conflict with other school activities. These would include, but are not limited to, exam week for termination of courses in progress, vacations, and extracurricular activities such as proms and sports events. Students tend to underestimate their physical stamina and do not take into consideration the fact that physical exhaustion impacts mental function. Conditions beyond the control of the counselor include the stress level of the student, the atmosphere at home, and social interactions students are having with peers that may have erupted immediately before the exam.

Preparation of the Test Taker- This includes both academic preparation (if an achievement test is to be administered) and the preparation given to the student about the mechanics of the test. Motivation to do well on the exam is also an important part of preparation.

Validity of the Test - If the test does not test what it is supposed to test, there is no reason to administer the exam. It is not only a waste of the student's and counselor's time, but it is detrimental to the motivation of the student in sitting for future tests. There is also the added danger of using incorrect and invalid results to determine future goals and placements.

SKILL 2.3   Major Functions of Appraisal

Assessment can take many forms and serve different purposes. The primary purpose of appraisal is to assist the counselor in helping students recognize their resources, utilize their strengths and accept their limitations, whether the focus is academic, social, personal or vocational. Increasingly, tests are used to measure student performance for reasons other than helping individual students with their educational and career goals. Nonetheless, it is the task of the counselor to assist the student in using all test results for self-understanding and growth.

Formal Assessment Tools

A variety of instruments are used for evaluation purposes. Formal tools with standardized scoring include tests administered by school counselors and other personnel as well as tests administered by the school psychologist. The school psychologist might utilize intelligence tests, which assess the ability to learn, as well as other psychological and aptitude tests in order to determine appropriate placement and develop individualized educational plans when needed.

School counselors, teachers and others may administer achievement tests (which evaluate how much has been learned), tests from the Georgia Student Assessment program measuring student performance, college entrance and preparatory tests (such as SAT, PSAT, and ACT), advanced placement (AP) tests, and others. These tests, while administered at school, are scored offsite by the testing company who prepares and distributes the tests.

Other formal means of appraisal include inventories that measure aptitude, vocational interests, personality traits, and learning styles. Many of these are scored by the school counselor or other personnel administering the test. Counselors may also use assessment tools designed to hone in on behavioral issues such as the incomplete sentence test, lethality inventories, suicide risk assessments, and depression inventories. These need to be used with caution and only with appropriate background and training.

Informal Assessment Tools

School counselors may find they use more informal means of assessment on a more frequent basis. These may involve using some of the inventories mentioned above as discussion tools rather than as formal assessments, behavioral observation of the student in the classroom or other settings, feedback forms developed to evaluate specialized guidance programs, behavior surveys, and needs assessments. The value of all informal assessment tools lies in their ability to give the counselor information that can enhance his or her work with students, and, in many cases, increase the student's self-awareness.

Appraisal can be used for these purposes:

1. To help students recognize and utilize the resources within themselves.

2. To improve self-understanding and to enhance self-concepts.

3. To assess the student's behavior and help the counselor and student anticipate the student's future behavior.

4. To stimulate the student to consider new interests for further exploration and to develop realistic expectations.

5. To provide meaningful information that can help the student makel intelligent decisions.

6. To aid the counselor and student in identifying and developing future options.

Appraisal also has limitations. These include the following:

1. The use of tests can, at times, interfere with the relationship the counselor has developed with the student, especially if the student is sensitive to being evaluated.

2. There may be a tendency to allow test results to dictate a course of action without considering many other factors. Care needs to be taken not to make assumptions about the student's abilities and choices based on testing alone.

3. If the results of the test are not presented to the student in a manner that promotes self-understanding, more damage than good can result from taking the test.

4. The use of tests tends to put the counselor in the position of an authority, so the student may perceive the test results as the absolute truth.

5. Many informal assessment tools, while helpful in generating discussion, can be used subjectively by both the counselor and the student.

SKILL 2.4   Procedures Involved in Appraisal Administration

Tests should be administered when the student feels the need for additional information for decision making. The parent or other interested parties should not make the decision. If the student makes the decision, motivation is high and this enhances the test accuracy.

When the test materials are received by the administrator of the test, they should be counted and the amount compared to the number on the invoice in order to insure the accuracy of the number of tests received. If possible, they should be placed in a safe with a combination lock known only to a few trusted school personnel. If this is not possible they should be put under locked storage in an area of the school that is not accessible to students and non authorized personnel.

A day or so before the test, the exams should be counted again to confirm that the tests have been kept secure. The tests should be divided according to the room setup and the number of students to be tested. They should then be replaced in the safe location and not taken out until shortly before the test is to be administered. At that time there should be a person in authority present with the tests at all times. Tests should never be left in a room without a proctor. When the students are given a test break, the tests should be closed and the room locked when the students leave.

After the exam is completed the following procedures should be adhered to:

A. Collecting

The proctor should count each exam and answer sheet as it is being collected. If the tests are numbered, each numbered test should be accounted for in order to insure two tests were not given out inadvertently. The students should not leave the room until all the exams and answer sheets are in order.

B. Storing

The tests should be placed in the safe location until it is time for scoring. If the tests are to be returned to the testing company for scoring they should be packaged immediately and prepared for mailing. The service selected for transportation should be notified and a pick-up date should be scheduled as soon as possible. In the meantime the packaged material should be placed in the safe location until picked up for transportation.

C. Safeguarding Data and Testing Instruments

As mentioned, the testing material should be kept confidential at all times until the counselor is released from the responsibility of protecting the tests or when it becomes the responsibility of other professionals. Access to the data results should be available only to authorized personnel. This includes the counselor, the parent/guardian, the student, and possibly a teacher or other school personnel or administrator. If individuals outside the school community (such as the media or an attorney) want access to the information, permission must be obtained in writing from the student (or parent/guardian if the student is a minor). The information could also be released by a court order if necessary. Legally, the counselor has no authorization to give any information about a student without such permission.

SKILL 2.5   Reporting Assessment Results to Students and Parents

The role of the counselor is not only to supply information to the authorized people concerned with the results of tests, but to be certain the results are interpreted and understood as accurately as possible. The communication of the test results should involve interacting and responding to the feelings and concerns of the student and his/her parent/guardian(s). Test results can be threatening to students and parents. They often feel results are absolutes and reflect a rigid evaluation of the student. Sensitivity to the feelings and needs of the student and the parent are primary in communicating results.

Since counseling is a confidential relationship, the counselor should obtain permission from the student to reveal any information given in confidence. This may sometimes apply to test scores given to parent/guardian(s). At the least, notification to the student that the parent will be receiving the scores and a verbal approval should be obtained.

Once it is clear that the parents are to receive the test report, the counselor should work with the parent in a counseling relationship. Parent/guardian(s) may not react objectively to the child's test results. If they do not agree that the results are consistent with their concept of the child's ability, it may be difficult for them to accept the results. Nevertheless, parents have a right to know, and, to best help their child, need the opportunity to see realistically the abilities of their child. In communicating with the parents, the counselor must be empathetic about the difficulty of accepting new information, and recognize the understanding level of the parent and communicate at that level.

The following techniques of test interpretation are useful in communication.

1. **The interpretation should be related to the goals of the counseling.**
All counselor-student relationships are based upon the needs of the student and his/her individuality. Therefore, sharing test data should be framed in this context. The student should be prepared and ready to receive the information and relate it, with the help of the counselor, to the predetermined goals of testing.

2. **The results of the test belong to the student.**
The goal of testing is to enhance the student's understanding of his/her interests, capabilities, and behavior. The student is entitled to the test results in a timely manner and there should not be a hesitation on the part of the counselor to withhold unfavorable results. Facing the reality of one's abilities is part of the maturation process. This cannot occur if the truth is not communicated or is colored in a manner that could be misinterpreted.

3. **The perception of the student to the scores is of the utmost importance.**
If the testing results conflict with self perception, the student could have emotional difficulties in accepting the information. This is where the skill and experience of the counselor comes into play. The goal of the counselor is to help the student and parents accept the information and build upon this new data. The counselor can enhance the likelihood of acceptance by striving to frame the all information (even seemingly negative results) as useful and instructive.

4. Provision should be made for individual interpretation.

It is preferable to interpret test results individually, but often the nature of the test and the number of individuals tested does not lend itself to individual counseling. When group interpretation is required, it is desirable to impress upon the students that individual consultation about their scores is available. In the group setting, the procedure is limited to explaining the purpose of the test and the norm group to which the students have been compared. Individual results should never be announced in the group. Statistics as to what scores are in different stanines or other ranges should be explained so students can evaluate their own results. The counselor should plan on conferring with individual students whose scores are low or whom the counselor knows will be concerned about their scores or when testing is the result of the counseling process.

5. The counselor must be thoroughly familiar with the test.

If the counselor does not understand the significance of the test results, accurate interpretation of the results cannot be expected. Therefore, it is imperative for accuracy as well as credibility purposes that the counselor is thoroughly familiar with the test that has been administered.

6. Interpretation sessions should be structured.

The purpose of structuring is to do away with the mystery of the testing situation, to help the student identify and correct mistaken impressions and to face some realities the results may reveal. Other issues of concern to the student and the parent/guardian(s) should be addressed at another interview, if possible.

7. Test results, not scores, should be communicated at a meaningful level to the student.

The purpose of reporting test results instead of scores is to help students use the information to form more realistic self-concepts. Scores in and of themselves do not impart information about the test taker. The student should understand the implications the results may have for the future. If the student does not understand the information presented, the most accurate information can be useless. Objectivity is the goal of the counselor in presenting the information, so counselor judgments and opinions should not be part of the process. It is also important the counselor explain the language used in the test results, the norming group to which the comparison is being made and the relationship between the score and the present and future goals of the student.

8. The student should help in the interpretation of the results.

This participation allows the counselor to see if the student understands the test results, encourages the student to contribute new information about him/herself into the counseling process, and tends to make the results more acceptable to the student.

9. Test results should, if possible, be verified by other information.
These data could consist of information from others who are familiar with the student as well as information from the students themselves.

10. The counselor, above all, must present the data and results honestly.
If the counselor suspects the student is disappointed with the results, the counselor must make an effort to support the student and explore the student's needs in light of the test results. Additional personal counseling sessions may be in order.

Test results should be retained either for use at another time, for comparison purposes or be made available to parents and others working with the student. Therefore a written record or report should be created. Results must be converted into an understandable form. The language of testing should be reported in the written report to insure consistency in interpretation by all professionals using the data. When a written report is given, it should be presented in a format that is understandable to the person receiving that report; whether it is one highly trained in interpretation, one moderately trained or someone with no training at all. In all cases, dissemination of test results should be on a "need to know" basis and only with the required permission.

There are many ways a written report can be created. These include, but are not limited to, a narrative format delineating the past and present record of the student, a graph form such as horizontal or bar graphs, or as a profile chart.

SKILL 2.6 Understanding the Statistics Essential for Interpretation

Since many professionals will be referring to the results of tests administered by the counselor and others, it is important that a uniform method of recording be employed. If a counselor records information in terms of percentiles, quotients, standard scores or stanines, it must be recorded accurately, easily understood and readily interpreted so the person receiving the score has the same interpretation as the person sending the score. The recording of the scores should also be consistent in that they are reported in the same language at all times.

Students must also be able to clearly understand the significance of their scores in order to make intelligent decisions based upon the results. For students it is not advisable to go into technical detail. They should know how their score compares with other scores of the group tested, as well as a comparison in terms of age, experience and general characteristics. They must also be familiar with what the test is supposed to measure, how effective it is, and some of the limitations of the test. A number score by itself does not have meaning if not related to these factors.

SKILL 2.7 Sharing Data with Other Professionals both Inside and Outside the School

The counselor must make every effort to safeguard this assessment results. School personnel should not have access to such data unless they are directly involved in providing services to the student, such as the school psychologist, special education teacher or school social worker. Generally, a need-to-know basis is the guideline. Under most circumstances, clerical staff, teachers and others should not have access.

While psychotherapists, social workers and other professionals outside the school who are involved with the student are bound by the ethics of confidentiality to which the counselor is bound, this material cannot be released with the express written permission of the student and/or parent/guardian(s). Once a release is obtained, all material relating to the student sent to these people should contain whatever is necessary for the recipient to help the student.

Test scores can be reported directly, as well as the counselor's interpretation of these scores and observations of the student when the scores were presented. This interpretation requires knowledge of the test, its structure and intent, and the scoring guidelines even if the scoring was done offsite. Such information needs to be direct and focused, and should not contain speculation or opinion not based on data. It is particularly important for counselors to be cautious in sharing the results of informal assessment tools.

SKILL 2.8 Interpreting Student Data from Written Reports

The counselor quite often is on the receiving end of written reports about students from various sources. These can be from a reading clinic, a psychiatrist or psychologist, a social worker or a teacher. It is important that the counselor is knowledgeable about the material in the report and, if some of the material is not understandable, investigate further for clarification. If the counselor is to counsel the student based upon these written reports, accuracy in interpretation is essential. Quite often it is appropriate for the counselor to seek a telephone or personal meeting with the writer in order to clarify and consult about the material in the report, as well as collaborate on an action or treatment plan.

COMPETENCY 2.0   SUMMARY

Correlation Coefficient - A statistical measure of the relationship between two factors.

Norming - The scores against which new scores are compared.

Raw Score - The basic score usually obtained by counting the number of answers right.

Reliability - The dependability or consistency of test results.

Reliability Coefficient - A statistical measurement of reliability.

Standard Deviation - The interval of score differences that indicates levels of achievement.

Standard Error of Measurement - The inaccuracy of a test caused by chance.

Standard Score - An indication of the distance between the raw score and the mean of the norm in terms of the standard deviation.

Standardization – provision that the test will be given and scored the same way at each administration.

Stanine - A measurement that runs from 1 to 9 and is a band of about one-half a standard deviation in width. Scores are based on percentile values.

Validity – Does the test measure what it is supposed to test? Includes face and content validity.

Conditions Affecting Test Results include testing room environment, physical, mental condition and preparation of the testee (including motivation.)

Major Functions of Tests: give information to help build realistic self-concepts, help students recognize strengths and accept vulnerabilities, develop realistic expectations.

The counselor's role in administering tests may include scheduling test dates, safeguarding tests, training proctors, and supervising test administration. Counselors must protect test score confidentiality. Test result interpretation must be accurate and fair.

COMPETENCY 3.0 KNOWLEDGE OF EDUCATIONAL AND CAREER DEVELOPMENT

SKILL 3.1 Similarities and Differences of Major Career Development Theories

There are five different classifications or methods of approach into which most major career counseling theories fall:

1) trait-factor theories
2) societal circumstances of career choice theory
3) developmental theories
4) personality and vocational choice theories and
5) environmental behavioral influences on career choice theories

The **trait-factor theories** assume there is a direct relationship between an individual's interests and abilities and vocational choices. When these are matched, the individual has found their future vocation. Interest inventories, aptitude tests and the general field of vocational testing have been generated from this theory.

The **societal circumstances of career choice theory** contends that circumstances of society, beyond the control of the individual, is the contributing factor in career choice. In this theory, the only control the individual has is in learning to cope with the environment.

The **developmental or self-concept theory** holds that as an individual grows older self-concept changes along with the view of the reality of his/her vocational choice. The satisfaction derived from the chosen career is based upon the individual's self-concept and the relation of that self-concept to the vocational choice.

The **personality and vocational choice theories** are based upon the concept that people of like personalities choose the same types of vocations. The needs of like personalities are the same and therefore they select the same vocations to satisfy those needs. The research done in this area has studied individuals who are already in a specific field as the norm group; their personalities are compared to those wishing to enter the field.

The **environmental behavior theory** incorporates elements of the societal circumstance and personality theories into a classification system that observes the relationship between the interaction of individuals in the environment and their behavior.
Most theorists in career development borrow from each other in formulating their theories. Some of key concepts of the most enduring theories follow:

1. **Bordin**, **Nachmann**, and **Segal** developed a framework for vocational development using a psychoanalytic theory base. By using the occupations of accounting, social work, and plumbing they attempted to generalize a system that might be used to classify occupations into areas of psychoanalytic dimensions.

2. **Ginzberg**, **Ginzberg**, **Axelrad** and **Herma** developed a theory that vocational choice is divided into three stages. The **fantasy period** is characterized by the lack of reality of the child in vocational choice. It is based on the child's imaginings and interests. The **tentative period** is characterized by a shift from the child's *interests* as they become aware that they have more *capacities* in one area than another. They then begin to consider these abilities in vocational choice. As they become older they begin to consider the *value* or satisfaction they get from some activities over others, and in the final stage they begin to incorporate all these subdivisions into the *transition period and* move into the **realistic period.** This period is divided into the *exploration stage* when all the elements of the tentative period are incorporated, with the added insight of what is feasible for the individual. These results come together in the *crystallization stage* that finally leads to the *stage of specification* where the individual finally makes a choice of a specific occupation. The theory is based on the general concepts of developmental psychology.

3. **Holland**'s theory of vocational personalities and work environments is based upon the individual's adjustment to six occupational environments and the interaction of those environments to the personalities of individuals.

The first of these six **occupational environments/personality types** is described as (1) *realistic*, portrayed by individuals who deal better with things than ideas or people, are oriented towards the present, and value tangible things such as money, power, and status. They avoid dealing with subjectivity and intellectualism, and lack social skills. They are persistent, mature and simple. These people are in the occupations of engineering, technical fields, skilled trades and agriculture.

The (2) *investigative* person thinks, organizes, understands, and copes with problems intellectually. They think themselves as intellectuals and scholars and tend to avoid interpersonal relationships. Their achievement is in academic and scientific areas. They hold less conventional attitudes and are found in occupations related to math and science.

The (3) *social* personality seeks satisfaction in therapeutic situations and is skilled in close interpersonal relations. They are sensitive to the needs of others. They are involved in teaching, understanding others, helping others by using their verbal and social skills for behavior changes, and are optimistic, scholarly and verbally oriented. They are found in the helping occupations.

The (4) *conventional* personality values rules and regulations, has a great deal of self-control, is neat and organized, and needs structure and order. They think of themselves as conforming and orderly. They identify with power and status but do not necessarily aspire to obtain those for themselves. They follow orders well. They are found in accounting, business and clerical vocations.

(5) Enterprising individuals are skilled verbally but use these skills for manipulation and domination and aspire to obtain power and status. They are aggressive, self-confident, verbal and social. Political, leadership and power roles are important to them and they aspire to obtain these roles. They are found in occupations of sales, supervision and leadership.

Finally the (6) *artistic* personality relates with others through artistic expression, dislikes structure, and relies on feelings and imagination. They think of themselves as intuitive, introspective, nonconforming, and independent. They value artistic qualities and are not interested in politics. They relate by the use of their artistic abilities. They are found in the arts, music, literature and creative areas.

The characteristics of the environments the above personalities seek closely resemble their traits and therefore dominate the work environment. It follows then that people seek out the work environments that suit their personalities.

4. **Roe** developed the concept that every individual inherits certain ways of expending their energies. This, combined with childhood experiences, results in a style that manifests itself in vocational choices. She draws on the needs theory of Maslow (webspace.ship.edu/cgboer/maslow.html) as well. The concept of genetic disposition together with needs theory and the influence of childhood experiences and innate style come together to form the basis of vocational choice.

5. **Super**'s theory of vocational behavior is based on the development of a vocational self-concept. This theory emerges from developmental psychology and behavior theory in relation to self-concept. He proposes that people express their self-concepts by entering occupations they perceive to allow self-expression. Individuals behavior in order to enhance their self-concept; different behaviors occur as a result of their present stage of life development. As the individual matures the self-concept becomes stable, but external conditions contribute to how that self-concept is expressed vocationally.

   Super explored the developmental life stages of the individual in reference to vocational behavior. These stages are similar to Ginzberg's classifications. They include *crystallization, specification, implementation, stabilization*, and, finally, *consolidation.* The adolescent is in the explorer stage in search of a career direction, the young adult seeks job training and job seeking, and the mature adult finds a vocation and secures a position.

6. **Tiedman** and his colleagues saw career development as a result of the developing self. The components include situational, societal and biological factors. The decision making process involves anticipation, implementation and adjustment. The sequence is characterized by an initial level of disorganized thinking about vocations, followed by clearer thinking and then evaluation of the advantages, disadvantages and values of each vocation. Teidman believes the career decision making process to evolve from the relationship between work and non-work activities.

There are many similarities in the theories of vocational choice:

1. Most of the theories are constructive; they describe the nature of the relationship between the person and vocational choice between two sets of observations.

2. The theories are generally descriptive rather than explanatory.

3. There is a great similarity in their explanations.

4. The research has not been experimental. Rather, these theories sort by groups and predict vocational choice based on characteristics of that group.

5. Most of the theories have roots in personality theory.

6. The theories are generally simple and uncomplicated.

There are also some differences:

1. Each of the theories states a particular set of objectives the individual is trying to accomplish through vocational choice.

2. Some theories have sufficient empirical data to support them and others have little empirical support.

3. There is a difference in when the most significant experiences for career development occur and what the critical sources of influence are.

4. The role of aptitudes is given various degrees of influence on career choice by the different theorists.

5. The role of family influence on career choice is treated with varying degrees of importance.

Generally the similarities among the theories are greater than the differences. They emphasize the same types of critical periods in career development and have their roots in personality theory. The differences lie in the choice of emphasis, the research methods appropriate for use in each theory, and the degree to which the relationship between various events occur.

SKILL 3.2 Career Development Activities

The counselor has the opportunity to create activities for students that help in career decisions. Recent expansion of computer generated career programs can be a starting point for these activities.

Career Day

Community resources are always available to aid the counselor in presenting real life career situations. The organization of the career day program is a time-consuming activity but it offers many opportunities for both the student and the counselor. The counselor makes valuable contacts in the community for future jobs for the students, for creating business relationships to help students and for enhancing the image of the school. Community business institutions are eager to influence young people to enter their professions in order to create a pool of future applicants. The student has in place a wealth of occupational information and can hone in on the areas of most interest. The students can also make their own contacts and make arrangements with the representative of the occupation of interest to them for further contacts. The counselor should take care to have a representative from each career cluster in order to draw students of varying abilities and interests.

Shadowing

Shadowing is the process of spending an extended period of time with a particular person or business in a field that the student is interested in as a possible future career. The student does not have to be fully committed to pursuing this career, but should have narrowed down the choices to a few specific careers so as not to waste the time of the person willing to help the student. The student should be given a set of rules to follow when chosen to participate and a form to fill out for an evaluation of the experience. The community business should also fill out a form prior to students presenting themselves. Questions such as what the business expects to get from the experience, how much time they are willing to spend with the student and their general practices should be included in the questionnaire. The business should also fill out an evaluation after the student has completed the shadowing experience. A bad experience on the part of the community volunteer might lead that person to not participate in the program the following year, and the counselor needs to know how the process went from the volunteer's perspective.

TEACHER CERTIFICATION STUDY GUIDE

Computer-Generated Career Inventories and Search Procedures

The state of Florida has written into its School Code, Chapter 239.124, 1994, the requirement that there be available to all students "Computer Assisted Student Advising". The code states that, "In conjunction with s. 240.2099 each public secondary school shall provide computer-assisted student advising through which students obtain information related to career descriptions and corresponding educational requirements, institutional admissions requirements for state universities, community colleges and area vocational-technical centers; and available sources of financial aid. Such advising must also enable students to examine their interests and aptitudes for the purpose of curricular and career planning."

The statute 240.2099 (1994) referred to in the above paragraph states as follows: "Computer Assisted Student Advising Network Plans - The Board of Regents and State Board of Community Colleges shall develop plans for implementing a computer-assisted student advising network statewide. It is intended that an advising network be developed for use by students enrolled in each of the state universities, community colleges, and public secondary schools. The implementation plan shall include, but not be limited to, the development of student-specific academic programs and an identification of information and services available to students through the network, the proposed utilization of student data available through the Florida Information Resource Network, the relationship of student enrollment patterns with plans for corresponding course offerings, the relationship of the network with the student registration process, the projected timetable for institutional availability of the network and any corresponding rules necessary to effect implementation of the network."

This statute puts in place CHOICES of Ottawa, Ontario, Canada, a commercial system that meets the requirements of the statute for students to explore and research different vocational and career choices. It can give them the ability to hone in on the occupations that are suited to their personalities and that conform with their academic achievement and interests. It is the responsibility of the counselor to become familiar with the network and to teach the student how to access the material. It is also the counselor's responsibility to help the student sift through the data received and further explore selected occupations through other means.

For the Florida counselor, this career decision program can be accessed through the Bureau of Career Development in The Florida State Department of Education. The state has an annual budget of $2 million for this Career Information Delivery System program to cover the mandate by the Board of Regents to the public school system for the institution of a far-reaching program of career development through the state educational system. A special feature of the system includes job listings in Florida as well as academic advising information.

Other computer-generated career information and exploration programs are available. Some of these include Career Information Systems (CIS), Guidance Information Systems (GIS), Systems of Interactive Guidance and Information (SIGI).

An excellent internet resource that is available to all counselors, as well as to families, is the Occupational Information Network (http://online.onetcenter.org.) Developed by the U.S. Department of Labor, this website provides accurate and updated information on careers, including occupational outlooks, earnings, and anticipated future growth, as well as a skills search, which helps to match users to appropriate jobs.

SKILL 3.3 Relate Decision Making Processes to Use in Various Aspects of Career Development

The process of decision making is used in all stages of career development. Although decision making in career development is a continuous process there are critical points that occur in the selection of an entry level job, a change of job or a change in educational plans.

H.B. Gelatt in 1962 advocated "a totally rational approach to making decisions." Since then, he has changed his view of decision making to being flexible, keeping an open mind, and using one's intuition. His definition of decision making is "the process of arranging and rearranging information into a course of action."

The three parts of Gelatt's decision making process are as follows:

1. Obtain the information that forms the basis for making the decision. All information can be biased by the fact that information is ever changing and is slanted by the sender of the information.

2. Arrange and rearrange this information by being flexible and having knowledge of your individual needs.

3. Make a choice. Try to be rational but if the decision seems irrational have a good reason for making that decision.

Tiedman and **O'Hara** have said that career choices are made by decision making processes that are subjective and depend upon the comprehension and control of the person making the decision. Their model tries to make the individual aware of all the factors involved in making the decision so they can make choices based on knowledge of themselves and of all the external factors involved. The process of decision making is divided into two phases. The first is the anticipation phase and the second is the accommodation phase. Each has several steps.

Anticipation Phase:
In the *exploration stage* the individual investigates all educational, occupational and personal alternatives. They identify interests and capabilities and consider the relationships among them and the alternatives suggested. The counselor provides support and teaching experiences as to the method of exploration and also provides career information.

In the *crystallization stage* the individual organizes, evaluates, synthesizes and orders the personal information and the alternatives from the exploration stage. Ideas are stabilized and formed as to possible career choices. The counselor helps in the organization, evaluation and synthesis of the information. Free discussion of issues and options continue to take place.

In the *choice stage* the individual makes a choice based upon the information gained in the crystallization stage with the consequences of the choice made as part of the process.

In the *clarification stage* the individual forms and carries out a plan to implement their choice. The counselor continues to supply information, support and feedback about the implementation of the choice.

Accommodation Phase:
In the *induction stage,* usually during the first months of the implementation of the choice, individuals come to understand the reality of the choice they have made. They begin to learn what is expected and required of them.

In the *reformation stage* individuals work out the realities of the choices they have made, become more comfortable with those choices and begin to rely less on the support and advice of the counselor.

In the *integration stage* of the decision making process, individuals integrate their identities with those in the choice setting and experience a sense of equilibrium.

Because decision making is a product of personality and values, it is important for the individual to have experiences that contribute to their emotional maturity, self-concept and values. Counselors should be the providers of information and resources about the use of that information so that an intelligent choice can be made. The counselor should also help individuals improve upon and perhaps learn different decision making strategies. Ultimately, once the necessary tools and resources are obtained, the decision is the responsibility of the individual.

SKILL 3.4 Evaluation of Educational and Career Materials

Guidelines for the preparation and evaluation of career and occupational literature have been formulated by the *National Career Development Association* (NCDA). These guidelines are appropriate for use in all vocational and education materials. Both publishers who create the information and users of the information follow these guidelines. They also serve as the basis for ratings of career and occupational literature by the *Career Information Review Service* of NCDA in the *Career Development Quarterly*.

General areas of evaluation should include:

1. *Dates of publication* in order to determine if the material is current. Material over five years old should be discarded as new information is usually available.

2. *Accuracy of information*, which is free from distortion and advertising. The material should be reviewed by trained experts in the evaluation process and reflect different points of view. Data should be based upon current and reliable research.

3. The *format* should be clear, concise and interesting.

4. The *vocabulary* should be appropriate to the age and level of the target group. Age ranges should be defined in presenting the material. Material targeted for young high school students, for example, should reflect appropriate language and style. The use of nonsexist language is important.

5. The *purpose of the information* should be presented in the introduction to the material and the target population should be clearly indicated.

6. *Bias and stereotyping* of individuals with a disability, or based upon gender, race, social status, ethnicity, age or religion should be carefully reviewed and deleted. Vocabulary should be gender-free and persons of both sexes should be portrayed equally.

7. The use of *graphics* is valuable but should be presented in a manner that is accurate, current, and unbiased as to sex, race, age and physical disabilities.

The content of all career materials should:

1. Describe the *duties and nature of the work* in a clear and interesting fashion. Literature describing the field should include the importance of the occupation in a global sense; the availability of the occupations; the skills, knowledge and abilities of members in the field; the different levels of occupations in the field; and the nature of any specializations.

2. Portray the *work setting and conditions* of the work environment in terms of the physical and mental duties of the work, the hours, required travel and any aspects of the work that might be considered undesirable.

3. Include the *preparation required* for entrance into the occupation, together with the training, knowledge, skills, and abilities of those successful in the occupation. The levels of preparation in each level of the occupation should also be described.

4. Delineate *special requirements or considerations* needed for employment in the occupation. These include bona fide physical requirements, licensing, and certification or membership requirements. Social and psychological factors that impact on one's lifestyle should also be addressed.

5. Describe a variety of *methods of entry* into the occupation.

6. Include information about *earnings and benefits.*

7. Portray *advancement possibilities* and the criteria for such advancement.

8. Address the long-term *employment outlook.* This is an important part of the evaluation.

9. Include *opportunities for experience and exploration* to ascertain if that field is appropriate for a specific individual.

10. Describe *related occupations* that share similar requirements.

11. Offer *additional sources of information.*

The National Career Development Association publishes a Career and Occupational Literature Reviewer's Rating Form that is available from NCDA, 5999 Stevenson Avenue, Alexandria, Va. 20034. This form can be used by guidance departments to rate material that is being considered for purchase for the guidance department or the library.

SKILL 3.5 Identification of Appropriate Materials for Educational and Career Development

There is much material developed for use in education and career development. It is the job of the counselor to be able to find useful information as needed for different students and varying needs. Becoming familiar with available references can help, followed by regular monitoring of new information. Career and occupational materials change quickly due to frequent shifts in the world of work and technological advances, so the school counselor must stay abreast of current materials.

Federal Governmental Sources

O*NET, a website run by the U.S. Department of Labor that provides helpful information about career trends to users at no cost. This site can be accessed through the Department of Labor's website for Education and Training Administration at www.doleta.gov/. Other sites and useful documents can be accessed here as well.

What follows is a list of useful resources from the federal government.

1. Employment & Training Administration, Department of Labor, *Dictionary of Occupational Titles (DOT)* - A comprehensive source of information about occupations and characteristics of the workers in individual occupations.

2. Employment & Training Administration, Department of Labor, *Selected Characteristics of Occupations Defined in the Dictionary of Occupational Titles.*

3. Employment & Training Administration, Department of Labor, *Guide for Occupational Exploration.*

4. Bureau of Labor Statistics, Department of Labor, *Occupational Outlook Handbook.* (Available online at www.bls.gov/oco/; updated every two years.)

5. Bureau of Labor Statistics, Department of Labor, *Occupational Outlook Quarterly.* (Available online at www.bls.gov/opub/ooq/ooqhome.htm.)

6. Department of Defense, *Military Career Guide.*

7. Office of Federal Statistical Policy & Standards, Department of Commerce, *Standard Occupational Classification Manual.*

8. Office of Management & Budget, Executive Office of the President, *Standard Industrial Classification Manual.*

9. National Center for Education Statistics, Department of Education, *A Classification of Industrial Programs.*

10. Bureau of the Census, Department of Commerce, *U.S. Census of Population 1990, Classified Index of Industries and Occupations.*

Other Governmental Sources

Regional sources include the *Bureau of Labor Statistics* regional center. Sources from the state of Florida can be obtained through the department of labor at www.floridajobs.org. Local sources include the chamber of commerce, the employment and rehabilitative services offices, community colleges and four year institutions, the private industry council (PIC), and civic or service organizations.

Commercial Sources of Information

There are many publishers who specialize in providing information about careers and vocations. Always evaluate their products using the guidelines noted in Skill 3.4 before utilizing these materials

SKILL 3.6   Interpret Student Appraisal Data Relevant to Career Development

Career development is a continuing process. It involves the evaluation of assessment results throughout the life span of an individual. Reflecting this concept, career counseling has grown from a trait-factor, counselor-dominated process to a developmental, client-centered process. This approach views assessment as a tool to increase self-awareness at every major transition period of the individual.

Objectives at each level of development enhance the growth of the individual, with one tool being the assessment instrument. The role of assessment in career development counseling has been recognized as important by the National Occupation Information Coordinating Committee (a federal interagency program) by establishing national guidelines for student and adult career development competencies. Go to www.ed.gov/pubs/TeachersGuide/noicc.html for more information and resources.

At the *elementary school* level, a career development objective might be increased self-awareness in relation to the world of work. This would entail the identification of personal interests, abilities, strengths and weaknesses as well as learning to value the benefits of education. Students could describe school activities that might help them be successful on a job as well as identifying academic skills needed in specific occupations of interest to the student.

At the *middle school* level, a career development objective might be to measure student preferences in different areas and their influence on the student's positive self-concept. This would entail that the student describe their personal likes and dislikes and to know of the benefits of education to career opportunities. The student should learn about his/her strengths and weaknesses in school subjects, what requirements and skills are needed for present and future occupations, the importance of academic and occupational skills in the working world, and the relationship of aptitudes and abilities to occupational groups.

At the *high school* level, it is important for the student to understand the relationship between educational success and work requirements, the role a positive self-concept plays in the world of work, and how individual characteristics relate to achieving life goals. At this level the student should be able to describe the relationship between academic and vocational skills to their own personal interests, ability and skills as well as how they can apply their own skills to present and future occupational needs.

Vernon Zunker, with influence from other theorists, has established a model for the use of assessment results in developmental career counseling. There are four major steps: analyzing needs, establishing the purpose of testing, determining the instruments to be used, and utilizing the results in decision making for training and education.
The four steps for using assessment results in career counseling are:

Analyze needs - A needs analysis should be conducted using biographical data, interviews, and educational and work records. The cooperation and participation of the individual in establishing their needs is important for the success of the results. To assist the counselor in identifying needs a *counseling relationship must be established* to help the student articulate his/her needs. The *acceptance and adoption of the student's views* will enhance the relationship as well as help in exploring their views in relation to realistic career goals. The *lifestyle needs* of the individual should be part of the needs assessment in order to relate the world of work to the student's values, recreational requirements, financial needs, family responsibilities and societal obligations. The *specific needs* of the individual for assessment should then be examined. A decision should be made as to the need for an assessment instrument.

Establish the purpose of testing - After the needs analysis is completed the counselor and student should decide the purpose of testing. Testing can be used for diagnosis, prediction and comparison of individuals with a normed group. Testing does not always meet all needs that have been identified. The purpose of testing can be specific, as in predicting success in an education or training program, or more general, as in establishing an overall direction of career exploration. The counselor should explain the purpose of each test to be administered as well as the desired results in relation to the stated needs.

Determine the instruments to be used - Tests to be used for career assessment should measure ability, achievement, career maturity, interests, personality and values. Achievement tests measure academic strengths and weaknesses. Career maturity inventories measure vocational development in reference to self-awareness, planning and decision making abilities. Interest tests compare the individual's interests with reference groups. Personality and value inventories reflect traits that influence behavior. Any of the test results can stimulate interaction between the counselor and the student about the relationship between work satisfaction and the actual work.

Utilize the results - The counselor and the student use the results of the assessments to discuss the unique individual characteristics of the student and their relation to career exploration. The test results are also used to help students view themselves as a whole person. Individual traits and characteristics are used to determine plans for the present and to look into the changing future.

SKILL 3.7 Assisting Students in Developing Employability Skills and Exploring Education and Training Options

School-to-Work Programs
One of the best ways to teach students to develop employability skills is to have the student participate in a supervised job experience. Motivation for the student to participate in this type of activity would be to incorporate it into the vocational curriculum and award high school credit to the student for successful completion of this component. Such school-to-work programs can be very useful.

Basic information about effective functioning in the world of work should be conveyed to the student. These include getting to the job on time, avoiding absences for all reasons other than illness, and calling the employer if one is ill and cannot report to work. Many students do not understand the importance of appearance and personal hygiene in obtaining and maintaining a job. These are basics that often have to be taught. In addition, many students have an attitude problem that has been carried over from school. Students need to understand that such attitudes are not tolerated in employment situations.

The instructional component of the school-to-work program should contain extensive material for the evaluation of the student by the employer as to attitude, work habits, personal hygiene, and attendance, as well as knowledge of the job and the ability and willingness to learn and be taught. Weekly work evaluation sheets completed by the employee and the employer show what the student has learned, and the conditions of employment that are satisfactory and those that need to be improved. There are many school-to-work programs that provide these evaluation instruments.

Exploring Career and Education Options

There are many methods of exploring career and educational options open to students. They include computer-generated career inventories, career and educational search materials, and specific information about careers and training requirements. There also are many career choice theories in place to help the counselor assist the student in identifying a career that will make going to a job each day a satisfying experience.

The role of the counselor in this task is to provide the information needed for an intelligent and realistic choice by the individual student. This entails providing information in a timely fashion at the stage of maturity and development the student has achieved, and following through with support to explore different avenues. Then the counselor can help students reach the next level in the decision making process: to choose the adult path of work that will provide a happy and fruitful work experience by meeting their economic, personal and social needs.

Educational and Vocational Training Opportunities

There are many opportunities for students to obtain work training and education besides the pursuit of a bachelor's degree. Often these other paths lead to higher paying positions in areas that are wide open for employment due to a lack of trained personnel in these areas. Some of these options follow.

1. *Vocational Education* - Often offered by public or regional area vocational centers in daytime, evening and weekend classes. These classes range from basic entry level programs to advanced classes to help students develop a variety of skills in fields such as computers, electricity and plumbing. If a student is of high school age the program is usually part of the high school curriculum. If the individual is of adult age the cost is usually low or there is an opportunity to obtain financial aid. See www.directoryofschools.com/North-American-Trade-Schools/Home.htm for more information.

2. *Community Colleges, Junior Colleges, & Vocational -Technical Colleges* - Most of these schools admit students who might not have the qualifications to enter a four year institution. This gives the student who is a late bloomer or has not done well in high school a second chance. Classes are scheduled so that individuals who may be holding full-time jobs can attend. The cost is usually reasonable and financial aid is available. The completion of these programs can lead to an associate degree, a certificate, a job promotion, or a new career.

3. *Private Career/Proprietary Schools* - These for-profit schools offer training in specific skill areas. They usually are more expensive than a public institution but have placement facilities. Financial aid is usually available. They are accredited by state and/or national groups. A guide to choosing a private career school is Myers and Scott's *Getting Skilled, Getting Ahead*.

4. *Apprenticeship Programs* - These are usually administered through a labor-union industrial council. Forty to fifty occupations are represented by classroom instruction and on-the-job training. The programs involve from two to six years. Contacts for apprenticeship programs can usually be made through the state employment office.

5. *On-the-Job Training-* These programs are similar to apprenticeship programs but are of shorter length and are usually part of a job orientation program for new employees.

6. *The Job Training Partnership Act (JTPA)* - This is an adult training or retraining program funded by the government and run by a local private industry council (PIC) in localities where there is a need for employment training in the area.

7. *Health Related Training* - This type of training is usually available at hospitals or hospital-related institutions where there is an opportunity for clinical or field study as part of the formal instruction.

8. *Military Service* - The military services offer training and continued training in fields that can be used after the individual leaves the service. The Reserve Officers' Training Corps (ROTC) program offers students the opportunity to receive up to a full scholarship for four years of study in exchange for an extended time in the military.

COMPETENCY 3.0 SUMMARY

Career counseling theories fall into 5 categories: **trait-factor, societal circumstances of career choice, developmental, personality and vocational choice**, and **environmental behavioral influences on career choice**.

The most well-known career theories are:

Ginzberg (1951) (Developmental) Three stages of career development: fantasy, tentative, and realistic. Career exploration leads to "crystallization."

Holland (1959) (Personality) RIASEC. Realistic, Investigative, Artistic, Social, Enterprising, Conventional.

Super (1953) (Developmental) Growth (roughly to age 11); Exploration (11-20); Establishment (20 to mid-adulthood); Maintenance (mid to late adulthood); Decline (late adulthood)

Gelatt (1962) proposed a decision-making model of career choice.

Tiedman (1963) Anticipation (exploration, crystallization, choice, clarification) and accommodation (induction, reformation, integration.)

Career Development Activities: Counselors are expected to help with such programs as Career Day, Job Shadowing Programs. Counselors should also be able to access and utilize computerized career information programs, which often include career assessments. The program currently used in Florida is called CHOICES.

O*NET is a website run by the U.S. Department of Labor that provides helpful information about career trends to users at no cost.

The National Career Development Association (NCDA) is a good resource for information on career counseling. Career information should be updated regularly; old information (more than 5 years) must be discarded.

Local information may be obtained through Chambers of Commerce, community colleges, and state rehabilitation or employment agencies.

COMPETENCY 4.0   KNOWLEDGE OF CONSULTATION

Skill 4.1   Components of a Consultation Prototype

The purpose of all consultation procedures is to problem-solve. The consultation process generally includes the consultant—usually the counselor in a school setting—but could also include a person knowledgeable about the problem at hand, and the consultee, often a teacher or other school professional. The consultee is not usually the student, whose problem is the topic of discussion. Certainly, the student has a vital part in the process, but the purpose of the consultation is to aid the consultee in solving a problem that usually concerns a student or a group of students. The persons involved as consultees are those who are seeking solutions to the problem of helping a student succeed. When students are the focus of problem solving, consultees can be one or more school personnel and consultants can be more than one person with knowledge of the student and/or expertise in the solving of this particular problem.

More and more, school problems have become global and will involve difficulties of a societal nature that affect the school environment and school population as a whole. Quite often, problems from outside the school setting spill over into the school, disrupting the learning atmosphere. The consultation model can also be used to attempt to solve school policy issues. Some examples of these issues are dress codes, drug policies, and issues of sudden death in the school community. Different approaches are often used, depending upon the particular goal or goals of the consultant and consultee. The consultation process is used most often when an academic problem of a student is the focus.

The consultant can take the role of an **advocate** in directly presenting evidence and attempting to persuade the consultee to take some form of stand or action. The advocacy can be in support of a student, group of students or of an idea to be implemented.

The consultant can also act in the capacity of an **expert** in a particular field. This role is employed when there is a need to inform or educate the consultee in a specialized area. For the school counselor, this can be in the form of interpretation of test data, psychological and environmental background or placement data. Another role of the consultant would entail specific **training and educating** in an area such as identifying "children at risk", with the goal of working out school-wide plans and procedures to solve the problem of the increasing rate of dropouts.

The counselor/consultant's role most often used in the school setting is that of **consultant/collaborator** where the consultee and the consultant's roles are equal in attempting to solve the problem. It is a three-pronged relationship; the counselor/consultant, the teacher/consultee and the client system (which can include the student and the student's parents). In the role as a collaborator, the counselor takes part of the responsibility for implementing the plan to solve the problem. The counselor may take on the role of directly working with the student to reinforce behavior change.

The task of **fact-finding,** or gathering information, studying it, and disseminating it to the consultee, falls upon the shoulders of the consultant. A consultant may also serve as a **facilitator** or **process specialist**, which is a specialist in the actual process of solving the problem by outlining the steps needed to reach mutual goals.

There is a common procedure for all consultation processes, although the settings in which the consultation takes place may differ. Some of these places are:

1. In a clinical setting which can be a mental health facility.

2. In a school setting with the parent, teacher or administrator present.

3. In a training setting for education purposes.

4. In consultation with the staff of an organization, be it school or business.

Background information as to the purpose and reasons for the consultation process, some of the political considerations of the process if applicable, and general information to aid the consultant in understanding the dynamics of the situation should be obtained prior to the first session.

The goals of the consultation should be formulated so that all parties concerned know the direction in which the process is headed. The function, role, techniques and procedures used by the consultant in the consultation process should be formulated after the above issues are determined.

The experience of the consultee in the consultation process should be taken into consideration so that if additional education and skill training are required, the consultant is prepared to furnish that training.

Some of the common procedures for all consultation processes are as follows:

A. Entry - Relationship Building

If we use the school setting as the basis for consultation, we most often are involved in attempting to change student behavior, be it in the area of classroom learning or abusive verbal or physical aggressive behavior. It is essential to obtain the trust and confidence of the student and to motivate the student to change.

The student, although not always directly involved in the strategies to be employed in attempting to change behavior, must be informed, instructed and must cooperate in the plans for implementing the behavior change. This is absolutely essential for the process to be successful. When this is done, the consultant can then contact other parties involved, such as the child's parents, teachers, experts in areas of special needs and any other support personnel deemed important in solving the problem.

The consultant will want to establish rapport with and between all parties. As far as possible, the student should be included in defining the problem with the consultee, especially at the secondary level, and should also be included in meetings of all parties concerned with formulating the strategies to be used.

B. Diagnosis and Defining of Problem

The problem to be solved should be clearly defined to all participants. Quite often, the consultee and the student see the problem in different lights and therefore a plan to solve the problem cannot work if the student is working at odds with the consultee. In a situation where a student needs to modify behavior, the model of **behavior consultation** is employed.

This method is based on the theory of social learning. The participants agree to seek specific changes in behavior. They obtain appropriate information regarding the problem, define the problem in detail, set goals, plan strategies, and explore and agree upon appropriate assessment criteria and avenues of intervention. It is important that the consultee is comfortable with the strategies that are agreed upon as the consultee is the main agent of change. Solving the problem depends upon the consultee "making it happen;" therefore, it is critical that the consultee has ownership of the plan.

Other models of consultation are **organization consultation** where the problem is in the organizational framework. This is most often used when an expert in that particular area is required. The **doctor/patient** model is used when an organization knows there is a problem but does not know the nature of the problem. When the interactions of the members of an organization are examined, **process consultation** is employed. When the mental health of a community can be improved by consulting with other human services professionals in the delivery of their services, **mental health** consultation is employed.

C. Devising and Implementing a Plan

In devising a plan, the counselor/consultant, together with the student and the consultee (teacher), identify a behavior that is of most concern to all. A plan of action is devised to expedite change with equal input from all participants involved. Techniques of encouragement, logical consequences, praise and reward are used to reach goals set down by all parties (this utilizes the Adlerian theory of behavior change). The consultant needs to monitor the process and identify problems with the implementation so as to devise changes in the plan if necessary.

D. Evaluation and Summarization

Although the initial meeting is usually not the only meeting, a designated notetaker should create a summary of what has transpired during the meeting before terminating the session. Each participant should fully understand their role in implementing behavior change and should be held responsible for their part in the process. At the end of the process of behavior change, an evaluation of the process should be made by the consultant.

Skill 4.2   Procedures for Assisting Participants in Problem Solving

The counselor/consultant should have a plan of action to assist the participants in doing their part in effecting change. This can take the role of teaching specific skills, as in the case of a teacher that has had no prior experience in attempting behavior change, or in helping the teacher devise strategies and sequential plans to deal with the behavior problem that has been defined. The consultant should be able to help the consultee describe in detail the specific types of behavior that are problematic. If necessary, the consultant should make arrangements for any clerical help needed in order to relieve the teacher/consultee of this task.

Help should also be provided to the student and his/her parents in order for the consultation to effect the desired change in behavior. This should take the form of frequent contact to evaluate the progress of the process and to ascertain if more help is needed or additional concerns on the part of the student and parent need attention.

Skill 4.3 Communicate the Needs of the Student

It is important for the consultant to clarify the student's needs directly with the student. In the case of an adolescent, if this is not done first, trust will not be attained and the whole process is doomed to failure. The counselor/consultant should obtain permission to share these needs from the student to reinforce the trust relationship. When this is done, the counselor/consultant should arrange a meeting with the consultee to communicate these needs. If the student can be present, in the case of an adolescent, no misunderstandings are likely to occur. This can also be a method to open lines of further dialogue between the student and the consultee. In this scenario, the consultant acts in part as the advocate of the student/client, using expertise acquired from experience. It is important the consultant balance the needs of the student/client with those of the consultee/teacher in order to achieve maximum results.

Skill 4.4 Communicate with Parents

Parents are a vital part of the consultation process. Given the increased awareness of parents in their child's school life and the advent of federal and state laws protecting the rights of the parents in school issues, the parents must be in on the consultation process from the beginning of the process. Even in the case of non-cooperative parents, the consultant must inform them every step of the way. Often, the situation is complicated by divorced and separated families, issues of custody, and alienation of the student from his family. The consultant, while respecting the parent's rights, must always keep in mind the primary goal of solving the student's problem.

The parent is a valuable source of information about the child. Issues of family background and medical history information can only be obtained from parents or those adults who have been privy to family interaction. Enlist the equal cooperation of parents by asking how they feel about suggested courses of treatment. Non-cooperative parents often enter the consultation interview with an "attitude" about how the school has "not done right by their child." It is in the best interest of all to permit them to vent their feelings. It may be one of the few times a school person has listened to them. Counselors will want to emphasize that the school is not giving up on the child, and that if past strategies for improvement have not worked, the school will continue to try. As soon as you can, focus on the issue at hand, explain the plan agreed upon to the parents, accept ideas for modification wherever possible and help them feel they are a vital part of making the plan work. Do not overwhelm them with too many tasks to perform, keeping in mind they may have too much stress in their daily lives already. Encourage them to feel this is a workable plan that may need modification as it progresses. It is important for the counselor to arrange a future time to make contact with them as to the progress of the plan. If additional contact is not made, the parents will feel negatively about the entire process and further intervention on the part of the school will be extremely difficult.

Skill 4.5 Assist in the Use of Data and Resources

The consultant needs to have as much information about the situation and the child as possible. Do not rush into the consultation process without doing an adequate job of gathering data. Some of the things the consultant can do are:

1. Examine the permanent record card for standardized test scores, patterns of grade fluctuation, weak and strong areas and attendance record.

2. Talk with the present teacher(s) to ascertain if they are all having the same problem, and if not, what can the teacher who is not having a problem contribute to the process.

3. Observe, if possible, the student in the classroom.

4. Administer additional tests if necessary.

5. Gather medical, physical and discipline history.

Once you have some kind of analysis of the possible problem, compile a list of resources that might be available, in and outside the school community, to be used as a support mechanism. This may involve long term personal counseling, both for the student and the family, alcohol and other drug counseling, academic tutoring, referral to the school psychologist for special education testing; and school social worker intervention for family visits and ongoing support. This list should be available when the consultation process begins, so if needed, action can be taken at that time.

Skill 4.6 Identify Procedures for Transition and Follow-Up

When it has been determined that the consultation process has been successful in intervening to solve the problem, a formal evaluation of the process is in order. This can be accomplished by a number of methods. Individual interviews with all parties involved in the process can be conducted with a survey instrument used to determine if the consultee and the student/client have been satisfied with the process, the areas they feel need to be continued or modified, the process for the continuation of the plan that had been in place, and any comments relating to the entire procedure.

The consultant becomes increasingly less active in the consultation process as part of the transition phase, agreeing to decrease and eliminate the need for intervention in a gradual way. As a final step, after the consultant has not been involved for a period of time, a follow-up interview should be conducted as to the effectiveness of the process. If there is a regression on the part of the student/client, it may be appropriate to reinstitute the consultation process or make further referrals.

TEACHER CERTIFICATION STUDY GUIDE

COMPETENCY 4.0   SUMMARY

Consultation: the purpose of consultation is to problem-solve by calling upon the expertise of knowledgeable parties. A consultant may be an advocate, an expert, a fact finder, or a facilitator. Counselors are likely to be consulted as experts for the interpretation of test data, psychological and environmental background data or placement data.

The Consultation Process Involves the Following Stages:

- Entry - Relationship Building
- Diagnosis and Defining of Problem
- Devising and Implementing a Plan
- Evaluation and Summarization

Communicate the Needs of the Student: The counselor will want to involve the student, as much as possible, in all stages of the consultation. This involvement increases trust.

Communicate with Parent/Guardian(s): Parents may be resistant to becoming involved with the school district's plans for trying to create behavior change, especially if they have had negative experiences in the past. Counselors must be sensitive to the parents' frustrations and keep them informed and involved throughout the process.

Assist in the Use of Data and Resources

During consultation, counselors will make reference to appropriate data and resources, including permanent records (seeking patterns of grade fluctuation), attendance records, relative strengths; teacher's reports; classroom observation; supplemental testing; disciplinary reports; and medical history. Counselors must also familiarize themselves with available resources in the school district and in the community, so as to be able to make appropriate referrals. Follow-up should always be done after a referral.

GUIDANCE AND COUNSELING

COMPETENCY 5.0   KNOWLEDGE OF COORDINATION

SKILL 5.1   Collect and Synthesize Student Referral Data

When a student is referred to the counselor it is important that all information about the problem and the reason for the referral is compiled so the counselor has a complete picture of the child and the history of the problem. Information should be received from all parties with knowledge of the child. This includes the parent/guardian(s), the teachers, and any support personnel who have been involved with the child such as reading and special education teachers, social workers, psychologists, and sometimes peers. When all this information is collected the counselor should analyze the data and come up with an initial approach to the student to discuss the problem. Additional referrals to other agencies or support personnel may be necessary.

SKILL 5.2   Formulate Referral Procedures for In-School and Out-of-School Individuals and Agencies

Appropriate referrals for students to professional individuals and agencies are procedural functions of both the school district and the specific school in which the counselor works. There is usually a set policy to which a referring counselor must conform. When the decision is made to refer a student for further help in solving a problem, all avenues of help should have be explored beforehand. For the in-school referral the counselor should evaluate the needs of the student in relation to the presenting problem. The usual scenario unfolds in this manner:

A student comes to the counselor to drop a subject because of failure. The course is required and the student needs to pass it in order to graduate. Dropping is not an option. The first step would be for the student, teacher, and counselor to meet to determine the reasons the student is not passing. There could be a number of reasons for the failure. Some of these are incomplete homework assignments, failure to come into review sessions when exams are scheduled, inability to understand the material of the course, frequent absences, and lack of interest or perceived irrelevancy of the subject matter. The counselor, teacher, and student choose the areas where help could be obtained. Some of these areas might be testing the student's reading ability, a general intelligence test to ascertain the student's level of ability in the area, instruction in study skills for the subject, and consultation with the parent/guardian to investigate the frequent absences. If referral to the school psychologist or the reading teacher, or special scheduled help sessions are recommended then the following procedure should be followed.

A form should be created, if not already part of the school policy, to inform the person to whom the student is referred the nature of the problem, along with background information, standardized test scores, what has been tried already, with whom, and what the results are of different strategies employed. Although this is an in-school referral the parents should be informed that a referral has been made and the reason for the referral. Follow-up and further meetings should be held to determine the outcome of the referral. The person to whom the student is referred should also issue a report on the results.

A scenario where the need for an out-of-school referral is necessitated might be the case of a student who, in the course of counseling, reveals sexual or other abuse, or the presence of an alcohol or other drug problem. The first step in getting outside help for the student, after all internal help has been exhausted, is to get the informed consent of the student and his/her parent/guardian to make the referral. In the case of sexual or other abuse by a family or household member, the counselor is mandated to report the incident to the proper authorities as well. If a parent or guardian is the abuser it is not prudent to include that person in the referral process. The mandated state organization will approach the parent.

In the case of alcohol or other drug or emotional problem, the parent/guardian should be included from the start. The question of expense or insurance coverage is a significant factor to be considered. In any case of referral, written documentation should be kept. Personal contact with the agency receiving the referral should be made by the counselor. Regular contact with this individual and the parents should be made until the problem is resolved or the student is no longer enrolled in the school.

SKILL 5.3 Informing the Community of Guidance Services

Quite often the community does not know the extensive functions of the guidance program. Some of the techniques that can be used to inform the community of guidance services and programs are as follows.

1. The guidance newsletter is an excellent vehicle to advertise what is going on in the guidance department and to systematically explain each program on a monthly and ongoing basis.

2. Writing a column in the local newspaper is an effective way to reach community members who do not have students in school.

3. Individual staff members may take turns in speaking to local organizations at their regularly scheduled meetings. These organizations are frequently looking for no-cost speakers to bring members to meetings.

4. Teas and orientations for parents of specific grade level students allow counselors to explain what programs are planned for their students during the school year.

5. Participation or attendance at athletic events and other out-of-school functions help counselors become visible to a greater portion of the school population and their parent/guardian(s).

6. When counselors invite community leaders to brain-storm on ways to help students succeed in a chosen field, this increases community awareness of the guidance program. The career night is a good example of this type of activity.

SKILL 5.4   Organizing and Administrating the Guidance Program

To support the activities of an organized guidance and counseling program, the resources of trained personnel, adequate facilities, and basic materials are needed. In the analysis of a guidance and counseling program the following components must be considered.

1. The program must be organized, have established systems of operation, and a stated purpose, along with trained professionals to administer the services.

2. The guidance service must be an accepted and integral part of the school program.

3. The mission statement of the guidance and counseling program should include the promotion of optimum student development and adjustment, with the ultimate goal of developing the child's ability to make intelligent choices and be able to deal with and solve the problems of life.

4. The services to be delivered should include, as a minimum, testing and keeping of appropriate records, personal counseling, the provision of educational and vocational information, appropriate placement into school programs, referrals to outside agencies and professionals, and follow-up of the services provided.

5. The program should provide for identification, exploration and development of the potential inherent in all individuals.

The ultimate aims of a guidance program include the successful acquisition by the student of academic and personal insights in order to make plans for the future with confidence and logic, to obtain personal satisfaction in acquired accomplishments, to make emotional adjustments, to be able to solve adverse problems as they inevitably occur in life, and to explore vocational and career possibilities intelligently and knowledgeably.

There are many ways to structure the guidance program. The director in charge of leading the program should include the staff in making decisions about the type of services to be delivered, the components of those services, and the staff assignment of those components which are consistent with the mission statement of the department. The staff member who is assigned specific duties should have the leeway to decide the components of the service and the method of delivery.

An important part of the success of the guidance program is an informed and supportive school staff, community and student population. The public relations involved in obtaining this support can be time-consuming but ultimately is both rewarding to the counselor and beneficial to students in all areas of their growth and development.

The results of the support of those other than the guidance staff in the delivery of guidance services contribute to the optimum functioning of the department and ultimately to the benefit of the students. To promote the guidance department, counselors can do the following:

1. Encourage cooperation between and among the guidance staff, the school staff, the community and the students. A special effort should be made to let teachers and others know that their roles in educating, guiding and counseling all students are vital to the success of the program.

2. Help develop a positive attitude by treating other school colleagues with respect. It may also be helpful to offer workshops and seminars on the functions and specific duties of the guidance staff.

3. Have a well organized program of regular parental contact. This could involve home visits or an advisory committee in which to bounce off solutions to problems, and the discussion and exploration of the feasibility of new programs.

4. Support community projects with a guidance context related to the needs and welfare of children.

5. Solicit the assistance of community leaders to offer mentoring, job shadowing and school-to-work programs.

6. Cooperate in establishing research projects directly related to proven scientific data for the instituting of program decisions and changes.

7. Continuously look for opportunities to promote the guidance program in innovative and unique ways.

SKILL 5.5 Creating an Orientation Program for Students to the School and Guidance Program

A major change in the life of a child is the transition from home to school. For the student entering school for the first time, as well as the transitions from elementary to middle school, and middle school to high school, a smooth and anxiety-reducing procedure can be extremely useful. While the attitude of the parent/guardian is important, the school people the child has first contact with sets the tone for the school experience. Therefore, it is important that the organizers of the first encounter recognize the needs of the child and address these fears and needs through a student orientation.

Careful planning is essential. There should be a written procedure to eliminate the possibility of omitting details important to the success of the orientation. They include:

1. Parents should receive advance notification of the time, date, and place of the orientation. The notice should include a student handbook with the school regulations clearly spelled out as well as penalties for infractions of the school rules.

2. The time should be set in the early evening and last for no more than an hour and one half.

3. The agenda for the meeting should be carefully delineated.

4. The principal and other school administrators should be introduced, and their role in the school community explained.

5. The Guidance Department should introduce its staff members, explain the functions and programs of the department, and the procedures for seeing a counselor.

6. There should be a question and answer period that is restricted in duration.

7. At the middle and high school levels, an explanation of the student's schedule should made with each student getting a copy of their schedule. Additional copies should be available on the first day for the students who have not brought their copy to school.

8. A tour of the facilities should be conducted by upper class students to help the new students familiarize themselves with the building and the rooms in which their classes will be held.

9. If possible, refreshments should be served with parents, students, and staff mingling in an informal atmosphere.

COMPETENCY 5.0   SUMMARY

Information Gathering and Coordination

The counselor needs to be able to gather information about students from many sources, including parents, teachers, support personnel, and peers. When referrals are made for additional help within the district, counselors should provide appropriate background information on the nature of the student's needs. This may include standardized test scores and attempted intervention strategies. Parents should be consulted with regarding referrals. Counselors should follow-up with students after making referrals.

Out-of-school referrals are necessary for cases of suspected abuse, substance abuse, or serious mental health problems. First, the counselor must obtain informed consent of the student and parents (except in the case of suspected child or sexual abuse, which must be reported to the proper authorities.)

Key Elements of an Effective Guidance Program:

- Guidance should be an integral part of the school program

- Basic services must include testing and keeping appropriate records, personal counseling, providing educational and vocational information, recommending appropriate course placements.

- Aims of a complete guidance program include equipping students with enough personal insight to make future plans with confidence and logic, helping students become emotionally well-adjusted, enabling students to face problems effectively, and assisting students in their explorations of vocational and career options and resources.

Ways to promote a strong guidance program: develop positive relationships with staff and students; maintain regular contact with parent/guardian(s); involve the community; be open to adapt to new needs; respect teachers, student and parents.

Orientation Programs: Guidance counselors should help to establish transition programs for students entering kindergarten, middle and high school. A well-organized program will have a clear agenda, including staff introductions, a question period, and an introduction to guidance programming.

COMPETENCY 6.0 KNOWLEDGE OF PROFESSIONAL, ETHICAL AND LEGAL CONSIDERATIONS

Skill 6.1 Legal Mandates and Ethical Standards Regarding Assessment Data

The Florida School Code, 1994, Chapter 232.248 "Confidentiality of Assessment Instruments", states that "All examination and assessment instruments, including developmental materials and work papers directly related thereto, which are prepared, prescribed, or administered pursuant to ss. 229.57, 232.245, 232.246, and 232.247, shall be confidential and exempt from the provision if s. 119,07(1), which exemption is subject to the Open Government Sunset Review Act in accordance with s. 119.14, and from ss. 229/781 and 230.331. Provisions governing access, maintenance, and destruction of such instruments and related materials shall be prescribed by rules of the state board."

Basically, this statute states that all assessment data generated in connection with the evaluation of a student are confidential and only to be viewed by school officials who have a "need to know". The counselor or other school official who has access to these records must obtain the written permission of the parent, guardian, pupil or student (who is over 18), to reveal them to any other person. For each request by others, the counselor is to obtain this written permission. Each state has their own regulations for legal and ethical standards of assessment but they all basically follow the pattern of this statute's provisions.

Skill 6.2 Professional Standards of the American School Counseling Association (ASCA) and American Counseling Association (ACA) (formerly AACD)

The ACA Code of Ethics and Standards of Practice were first developed in 1961 and revised in 1974. Since then, they were revised approximately every seven to ten years, the latest revision being in 2005. These codes are discussed below.

The Counseling Relationship
The relationship between counselors and clients is based on trust and respect. Therefore, counselor is responsible for respecting the dignity of all clients and always being mindful of the clients' welfare. The counselor must keep appropriate records, get informed consent, maintain professional boundaries, be culturally and developmentally competent, and be ever vigilant about avoiding harm to clients.

Confidentiality

It is important the counselors provide their services in a culturally competence manner that respects the rights of the client. Clients must be provided with information and guidelines by which the counselor may breech confidentiality. This informed consent may need to be reviewed throughout the counseling relationship. Records containing sensitive information about clients should be handled with the great care and discretion in location. Exceptions of confidentiality may include when clients are in danger of harming themselves or someone else and when the counselor's work with the client is court-ordered, with disclosure being a condition of the counseling. At all times, the counselor must make every effort to protect the information the client has disclosed within the confines of the trust-based relationship.

Professional Responsibility

Counselors must have a working knowledge of their ethical responsibilities as they work with clients. To best serve their clients, counselors need to know the extent of their competence (knowing when to refer a client to another provider), be involved with continued professional development, clearly and realistically publicize their services, fairly represent their professional qualifications, monitor the effectiveness of services rendered, and rigorously practice codes of conduct that are nondiscriminatory.

Relationships with other Professionals

Consultation is a powerful tool in the counseling practice. No counselor is expected nor should be expected to know how to work with all populations, cases, and presenting challenges. Establishing relationships with other professionals and specialists allows counselors to discuss the effectiveness of case management, maintain confidentiality, and to increase overall effectiveness of the services provided to the client.

Evaluation, Assessment, and Interpretation

Assessments may be related to education, career or psychological issues. Intended use of any instrument must be disclosed to the client. Multicultural considerations are taken into account to avoid assessments that are inappropriate due to a biased empirical background. Part of counselors' continued professional development is to ensure that any assessment used is the most recent version available. Legal proceedings for forensic evaluations can include that of the professional opinion of the counselor as well as written or court-ordered consent.

Teaching, Training, and Supervision

Consultation with professionals allows supervising counselors to ethically monitor the work of counselors-in-training. Before serving as a supervisor, counselors undergo extensive training in policy and procedures in the areas of appraisal and evaluation. Supervisors have an ethical obligation to the clients of the supervisee to ensure the services provided are appropriate. Supervisors need to encourage counselors-in-training to refrain from providing counseling and related services when their physical, mental and emotional well-being are called in to question.

Research and Publications

It is imperative that counselors establish and maintain ethical standards in conducting research. Participants must be notified of the purpose of the study, and how their input or results will be used, as well as receive information about the results of the overall project. Federal and state laws as well as institutional regulations need to be firmly adhered to.

Resolving Ethical Issues

Following ethical and professional standards is critical to the importance of the work counselors do with their clients. Ethical standards not only prevent harm to the client, but also protect the counselor from making unfounded and unintentional mistakes. Counselors need to consult with other counseling professionals about any situation or case that warrants an ethical question or decision. Should a counselor suspect a colleague of ethical misconduct, ACA expects counselors to follow the protocol as illustrated in the ACA Policy and Procedures for Processing Complaints of Ethical Violations.

These areas cover the most often questioned areas of ethical practice. They are by no means all-inclusive; instead, they are guidelines as to ethical behavior. Although the ethics are more specific than standards, they cannot possibly include all situations. Standards of practice are, by their nature, more generic and provide basic behavior standards for all counselors. These codes serve the purpose of identifying areas of concern, not of providing a "cook book recipe" as to standards of conduct or as to the resolution of specific ethical situations.

Professional counselors can be certified in different areas by the National Board of Certified Counselors (NBCC), as well as be licensed in their individual states. These certifying agents have their own code of ethics to which members are accountable. The counselor who holds each specific certification or license is ethically bound and accountable to know and abide by his or her ethical code. The counselor is bound by these codes, and violations can and should be reported to these monitoring agencies for potential consequences to the counselor.

When an issue of ethics arises in the counselor's practice, be it in private practice or in a school setting where the counselor is employed by an agency, it is wise to have one's own process of determining the course of action. Reference to the ACA Code of Ethics would be the first step in the resolution of the problem. Additionally, after formulating a course of action, all the ramifications of that course of action should be weighed. If there are any doubts as to the ethics of this course of action, colleagues, attorneys and specialists should be consulted.

In the past, divisions of ACA, such as ASCA, had their own code of ethics, but in 1997, with the revision of the Code, divisions were asked to dissolve their codes and develop Best Practice Guidelines as a basic coverage with specific codes that apply to their specialty areas. It is important, however, that school counselors model their guidance programs to reflect that of ASCA guidelines.

To view ACA's Code of Ethics or access resources related to ethical dilemmas, go to http://www.counseling.org/Resources/CodeOfEthics/TP/Home/CT2.aspx.

SKILL 6.3 Legal Rights of Students and Parents Concerning Student Records[D4][REC5]

School employees, on a need-to-know basis, may have access to student records. These individuals may include principals, assistant principals, school psychologists, school counselors, and special education professionals. Regardless of his or her position, each employee must maintain the confidentiality of student information.

In 1973, Congress passed a federal statute called FERPA to clarify the legal rights of students and parent/guardian(s) concerning access to student records. Also known as the "Buckley Amendment, FERPA stands for Family Educational Rights and Privacy Act (20 U.S.C. § 1232g; 34 CFR Part 99). (Go to http://nces.ed.gov/forum/FERPA_links.asp for more information about FERPA.)

Schools that receive funds from the federal government must comply with FERPA. The rights afforded by FERPA apply to parent/guardian(s) of students under the age of eighteen. Once a student turns eighteen, these rights are then transferred to the "eligible" student.

Under 34 CFR Part 99.7, FERPA states that parent/guardian(s) be notified on an annual basis about their rights to have access to or review their student's records. The following criteria must be included in the annual notification:

1. Parent/guardian(s) have the right to review their child's records
2. Parent/guardian(s) can advocate for changes to be made to the record should any information be incorrect.
3. Parent/guardian(s) can provide or withhold consent for the disclosure of personal information located with their child's record.

4. The way in which a parent/guardian can file a complaint with the Department of Education concerning a school or institution's failure to comply with FERPA.
5. Define which school officials that may have access to school records.

Schools may use a variety of ways to inform parents about their rights such as the school or community newspaper, bulletin boards, and student handbooks. Schools are not required to individually inform parents of their rights. Schools must procure parental consent to share student personal information. For example, a high school counselor must have a consent form on file before providing information to a college concerning a student's academic background. The ethical counselor will with hold providing personal information (except for information that has been published publicly, such as a student directory) to colleges, military recruiters, and coaches without gaining consent of the parent or guardian.

Skill 6.4 Knowledge of Use of Legislation in Regards to Special Needs Students

Special education law is filled with abbreviations. In the following explanations the abbreviations are used instead of the actual names of the acts or authorities. The following is a list of important abbreviations for easy reference. (See www.ed.gov for more information.)

EDGAR - Education Department General Administrative Regulations

EAHCA - Education for all Handicapped Children Act

EHA - Education for the Handicapped Act

FAPE - Free Appropriate Public Education

IEP - Individualized Education Program

IFSP - Individualized Family Service Plan

IDEA - Individuals with Disabilities Act

ITDA - Infants and Toddlers with Disabilities Act

LEA - Local Education Authority

OCR - Office of Civil Rights (U.S. Department of Education).

OSERS - Office of Special Education and Rehabilitative Services (U.S. Department of Education)

OSEP - Office of Special Education Programs (U.S. Department of Education)

SEA - State Education Authority

In 1975 Congress signed into law the Individuals with Disabilities Education Act (IDEA), or Public Law 94-142, making local and state education entities responsible for providing children with disabilities a "free and appropriate public education." This act was a turning point in the education of children with disabilities providing that these children have a right to FAPE and also provided for procedural protections to insure that they received this FAPE. Subsequently Section 504 of the Rehabilitation Act of 1993 was enacted and also affected educational rights of children with disabilities.

There are overlapping provisions as well as differences between these laws with Section 504 being broad and general, including a wider range of discrimination while IDEA is more specific and detailed. Other Acts delineate the delivery procedures of education services to children with disabilities.

Brown vs. Board of Education and Mills vs. Board of Education were two important legal decisions that helped hasten the enactment of education protections for children with disabilities. Section 504 of the Rehabilitation Act of 1993 provided that "No otherwise qualified handicapped individual ... shall solely by reason of his handicap be excluded from participation, in, be denied the benefits of, or be subjected to discrimination under any program or activity receiving federal assistance." The subsequent amendments provided for payment of costs of attorney's fees and damages to parents if they proved successful in legal suits brought against educational institutions for not providing their children with a FAPE.

IDEA is a funding vehicle of the Federal Government for a SEA to provide a FAPE to all children with disabilities. In addition if a state opts to provide a FAPE for children ages three to five and eighteen to twenty one, it must, under IDEA, provide that opportunity for all children with disabilities in those age groups. In addition if any children <u>without</u> disabilities in those age groups are provided with educational services, then a proportionate share of those with disabilities must also be provided with that educational service. The funding is provided by a complicated formula taking into account the number of children in a given state who have been classified as disabled.

Each state monitors the devising and implementing its own FAPE. The main provision enacted by Congress was the requirement that each child classified be provided with an IEP on an annual basis. Procedural protections include that the child be identified, evaluated by a multi-disciplinary team, eligibility for special education determined, and an IEP developed with parental participation.

According to Florida law, the legislative intent is to prevent handicapping conditions in young children and to minimize handicapping conditions that can not be prevented by "focusing prevention efforts on high-risk pregnant women and on high-risk and handicapped preschool children and their families. The Legislature further finds that by preventing handicaps in preschool children, infant mortality and child abuse can be reduced. The Legislature finds that infant mortality, handicapping conditions in young children, and other health problems for infants and mothers are associated with teenage pregnancy and that the prevention of sexual activity and unwanted teenage pregnancy can reduce the number of at-risk children, while increasing human potential and reducing the cost of health care... It is the intent of the Legislature, therefore, that a continuum of efficient and cost-effective prevention and early assistance services be identified, that a plan of intra-agency and interagency coordination be developed for the purpose of implementing such a continuum, and that the continuum of services be implemented as resources are made available for such implementation." (Florida School Laws 1996, Chapters 228-246, s. 411.22)

This statute provides for programs to help prevent teenage pregnancy, handicapping conditions and health risks brought on by insufficient education on the part of the families of children-at-risk, as an outgrowth of federal legislation. In addition, Florida School Laws 1996, chapter 411.243 addresses itself to a Teen Pregnancy Prevention Community Initiative. The main thrust of this community initiative is to "address current gaps in the comprehensive teen pregnancy prevention plan for communities." The main prevention components are:

1. Strategies targeting males.

2. Role modeling and monitoring.

3. Intervention strategies targeting abused or neglected children.

4. Human sexuality education.

5. Sexual advances protection education.

6. Reproductive health care.

7. Intervention strategies targeting younger siblings of teen mothers.

8. Community and Public awareness.

9. Innovative programs to facilitate prosecutions under s.794.001. s. 794.004, or 800.04.

Secondary prevention components are:

1. Home visiting.

2. Parent education, skill building, and supports systems.

3. Care coordination and case management.

4. Career development.

5. Goal setting and achievement.

The statue also provides for evaluation and technical assistance, training and quality assurance in carrying out the initiatives in achieving its goals.

All these statutes are in the domain of the guidance counselor at the secondary level. The counselor should be instrumental in implementing the programs that are created by these statutes as well as being the student advocate for helping to reach the targeted population.

Skill 6.5   Laws Regarding Child Abuse and Neglect

As an employee of the school board, counselors are required to report any cases in which they have knowledge of "child abuse or neglect or unlawful sexual offense". The law is clear on this issue, and, although the confidentiality of the counselor/client relationship may be violated, this is an example of the duty of the counselor to protect the minor child from harm. Most often, though, the child who is a victim of such abuse, and who reports it to the counselor, is seeking help. The skillful counselor seeks the consent of the child to report the incident or incidents in an effort to maintain a trusting relationship with the child.

Florida School Code
The following provisions of the Florida School Code regarding child abuse and neglect is similar other states in its regulations. The counselor should investigate the laws in the state in which he/she will be practicing in order to become familiar with the procedures to follow in reporting suspected cases.

Chapter 232.50 of the Florida School Code, 1994, states that every school board shall by March 1, 1985:

"1) Post in a prominent place in each school a notice that, pursuant to chapter 415, all employees or agents of the district school board have an affirmative duty to report all actual or suspected cases of child abuse or neglect, have immunity from liability if they report such cases in good faith, and have a duty to comply with child protective investigations and all other provisions of law relating to child abuse and neglect. The notice shall include the statewide toll-free telephone number of the state abuse registry. 2) Provide that the superintendent, or his designee, at the request of the Department of Health and Rehabilitative Services, will act as a liaison to the Department of Health and Rehabilitative Services and the child protective team, as defined in s.415.503, when in a case of suspected child abuse or neglect or an unlawful sexual offense involving a child the case is referred to such a team, except that this subsection may in no instance be construed as relieving or restricting the Department of Health and Rehabilitative Services from discharging its duty and responsibility under the law to investigate and report every suspected or actual case of child abuse or neglect or unlawful sexual offense involving a child."

"Each district school board shall comply with the provisions of this section and such board shall notify the Department of Education and the Department of Health and Rehabilitative Services of the compliance by March 1, 1985."

As an employee of the school board, counselors are required to report any cases in which they have knowledge of "child abuse or neglect or unlawful sexual offense". The law is clear on this issue, and, although the confidentiality of the counselor/client relationship may be violated, this is an example of the duty of the counselor to protect the minor child from harm. Most often, though, the child who is a victim of such abuse, and who reports it to the counselor, is seeking help. The skillful counselor should be able to get the consent of the child to report the incident or incidents. Regardless, counselors must inform students of their duty to report suspected abuse in order to maintain trusting relationships with students.

COMPETENCY 6.0   SUMMARY

Confidentiality: Must be maintained with the exception of clients who pose a danger to themselves or to others. Clients must be aware of these exceptions.

Professionalism: Counselors must not misrepresent their competence and refer clients when necessary. Clients must treat all clients in a nondiscriminatory fashion.

Evaluation, Assessment, and Interpretation: Assessments must be related to educational, career or psychological issues and their intended use must be disclosed.

Ethical Guidelines: Counselors must follow ethical guidelines when conducting research, including informed consent and refraining from causing harm.

Counselors should adhere to published ethical guidelines and consult with other counselor when faced with an ethical question. Counselors should report colleagues suspected of misconduct to professional associations.

Student records: Parents, guardians, and students have rights of access, rights of challenge and rights of privacy regarding student records. This includes all official records and files, including grades and standardized test scores, attendance data, and verified reports of behavior patterns.

Special Needs Students: Counselors must be aware of legislation pertaining to the specific rights of special needs children. Federal law (Individuals with Disabilities Education Act, IDEA) requires school to provide children with disabilities a "free and appropriate" public education. This includes Individualized Education Plans (IEP), which counselors often assist in developing and writing.

Laws Regarding Child Abuse and Neglect: School employees are required to report any cases in which they have knowledge of "child abuse or neglect or unlawful sexual offense." Counselors should have knowledge of the state child protection laws. This may involve breaking confidentiality. Counselors should be alert to the signs of abuse or neglect.

TEACHER CERTIFICATION STUDY GUIDE

COMPETENCY 7.0 KNOWLEDGE OF PLACEMENT

SKILL 7.1 Learning Styles and Individual Differences

Human learning is a complex human behavior and the way one learns is as individual and unique as each person. Different styles refer to the *preference* a person may have for learning in a particular way; this approach does not suggest that students can only learn in that way. In fact, exposure to varied learning approaches can be beneficial and growth-enhancing.

Research into learning styles has yielded eighteen different elements that contribute to various learning styles. In an attempt to classify this information, **Dunn** and **Dunn** isolated four different learning styles with varying components. These learning styles take into consideration the varied aspects of the way individuals learn. Further, Dunn and Dunn have developed a learning style inventory that assesses each of these elements.

The four major aspects of learning styles and learning environments are:

Environmental Elements: There are four environment elements that affect the way a student learns. These elements are part of the learning style of the student.

The element of *sound* varies with the learning. Some children can block out sound completely when studying and learning; others require complete silence. Others need only relative quiet and while still others must have a familiar sound, such as music or television, to block out extraneous noises that interrupt their train of thought. Still others can concentrate with or without sound, in silence or noise, or with any sound at all.

Light is also a factor in learning but not as critical as the element of sound. Some students need intensely bright lights in order to be comfortable in reading or writing and consequently become drowsy and lethargic in inadequate light. Some students prefer a subdued light to feel comfortable.

Tolerance to *temperature* varies greatly according to the individual. Concentration alters with the need for warmth or coolness, which can affect the degree of productivity of an individual.

The *design* of the study area is often critical to individual learning styles. Some students need an informal setting such as the floor or an easy chair. Others require a more formal setting such as a table or hard chair in order to concentrate adequately and for others there is no need to take into account the design of the site in which they study.

Emotional Elements: The emotional elements involved in the way a student learns also impacts on the quantity and quality of work produced.

The *motivated* student comes to the task with enthusiasm and excitement, asks questions and goes beyond the requirements of the class to explore further related areas. The *unmotivated* student cannot take in too much at one time, needs short assignments and requires the experience of success to continue to achieve. The unmotivated student will often respond to an individualized program of choices, teaming, or self-evaluation.

The trait of *persistence* is the ability to find the answer to a problem no matter how difficult. Persistent students will use resources or other students for help before asking the teacher for answers. They will not give up but continue to work on a problem until it is solved. Other students, such as those with short attention spans, find it difficult to maintain interest in the subject, daydream, become irritated or disruptive, and do not continue to attempt to solve problems for any period of time. These students need to have rules and objectives set out clearly.

The emotionally mature student shows signs of *responsibility* for the completion of the task at hand without constant supervision. Students who have difficulty learning because of reading problems become easily discouraged and need different methods of receiving material. They may need taped instruction, games, small groups or a structured multi-sensory learning packet. Their different learning styles do not conform to the expected norms.

The student who needs *structure* must have specific rules for the completion of an assignment. These include time limits, restriction of options, and a specific way of responding. Different students need different amounts of structure depending upon the learning style and ability to make decisions. The motivated, responsible and persistent student needs little structure while the unmotivated student with learning problems needs the most structure to achieve success.

Sociological Elements: The ability to learn varies with the student depending upon the atmosphere and individuals involved in the teaching situation. Students can learn from different individuals at different times and in different settings. These settings include learning from *peers, by oneself, in pairs or teams, with an adult or teacher, and in a mixed group.* How students learn sociologically can be determined by allowing them to choose their own method of studying and completing assignments with monitoring by the teacher to check on progress.

Physical Elements: The senses of *seeing, hearing, smelling, feeling* and *touching* are instrumental in the way many individuals learn. Those who learn through *visual* senses can see images in their mind; those who learn through their *auditory* senses learn by listening to sounds; those who learn by the *tactile approach* must be able to touch and feel in order to understand and those who learn through their *kinesthetic* senses need to have actual experiences with the shapes and forms of letters and words. Many students learn from a combination of some or all of the elements discussed.

Other physical elements involved in the process of learning include, the taking of food breaks or *intake, the optimum time of day or night*, and *the ability to move around at will.* Adjustments for these learning styles will produce the ideal atmosphere for learning.

Another theorist in learning styles is **Howard Gardner**. He has developed the idea of multiple intelligences. He posits that there are eight different kinds of intelligence and that each person is more or less inclined to demonstrate each of these. While this theory has engendered some debate in the field of education, it has opened up an important discussion about how schools can better respond to the diversity of students' learning styles. (For more information, see www.infed.org/thinkers/gardner.htm.) A multiple intelligence survey is available to assess a student's approach to learning.

In addition to the Dunn & Dunn Inventory and Gardner's multiple intelligence test, there are other learning style and personality inventories that can help determine the style or combination of styles suited to individual students. These include the Schmeck, Ribich, & Ramanaiah Inventory of Learning Process for information processing preferences, the Myers-Briggs Type Indicator for personality preferences, and the Kolb Learning Style Inventory. The assessment of a student who is having problems learning might give the teacher direction as to useful methods for motivating and encouraging a particular student to succeed.

Gender Differences and Learning Styles

Recent research and some educational practices have recently focused on differences in the ways girls and boys learn and function in the school environment. There is some indication that, as a group, boys tend to be more competitive and individualistic in their approach to learning, whereas girls are more inclined to work cooperatively with others, are more social, and are more interested in understanding ideas than in assessing facts.

Perhaps the most important thing for school counselors to remember is that gender (or other aspect of social identify such as race and ethnicity, immigration status or social class) is only one variable among a range of variables that contribute to the unique development and capabilities of a given individual. Further, differences within a given group (such as girls or boys) are almost always greater than the differences between two such groups. In other words, there is great variation among any given group of students and a range of individual and social factors contribute to these differences. Paying attention to each student's individual needs is the best approach to facilitating academic success.

See www.maec.org/beyond.html#learn and www.aauw.org/research/genderWars.cfm for more information about gender differences in the school environment.

SKILL 7.2 Post Secondary Educational Opportunities

The opportunity for additional education for all students is hampered only by motivation and abilities. Cost is also a major factor, but can be overcome by grants, loans, and scholarships. For the student who resides at home, the community college is an excellent start. This option can minimize the cost of financing an education or for those who have the motivation and ability but have not done well enough in high school to enter the university of their choice.

The U.S. Department of Labor puts out periodic reports on the availability of job opportunities for future years. (See **at http://www.doleta.gov/).** Students who have specific vocational choices should consult this report to determine if jobs in the field they are interested in will be available when they are ready to begin their work career. This information can help focus students' decisions about post-secondary education.

A. Vocational Training - Most states have a state university system that includes specialized schools which provide vocational training of students for entry level employment. Details about the program and the qualifications for entrance into that program are usually accessible through publications issued by the individual state education departments. (For information about Georgia's system, see http://www.georgiaencyclopedia.org/nge/Article.jsp?id=h-3292&hl=y.)

Barrons and *Peterson's* also put out publications for privately sponsored vocational programs. These sources of information should be available to students in the guidance office or the school library. Guidance in choosing these programs should be offered by the counselor when the student is called in for individual interviews in regard to future plans.

TEACHER CERTIFICATION STUDY GUIDE

B. College Education– Computer-based programs from *Guidance Information Services* and *Discover* are two of the many services offered for students who are looking for higher education opportunities and who have specific requirements in mind. The search for colleges should begin in the junior year of high school in order for the student to have narrowed down the choices to a manageable number when their senior year begins. The counselor should be interviewing junior students for this purpose when they are scheduled for senior year classes.

C. Military Service and Education – Students interested in entering the military will have the opportunity to take the ASVAB (Armed Services Vocational Aptitude Battery) to determine their areas of vocational abilities and skills. Military recruiters usually approach the guidance department early in order to interview potential candidates. They also contact students and parents at home to explain educational and enlistment benefits of the military service. The ROTC program enables a student to have a four year college education paid for by the government in exchange for future military service. This is an excellent opportunity for students who do not have available funds for college to receive an education and would also like to serve in the military.

SKILL 7.3 Locating and Securing Scholarship and Financial Aid Assistance

The guidance department should have a collection of books and information to help students locate and secure scholarships and financial aid. There are printed guides available, although many students and parent/guardian(s) find using the Internet most helpful.

There are many resources online. Although some commercial sites may provide useful information, they may not be the best or most unbiased sources, and some charge a fee. Two free non-commercial sites with good information are www.finaid.org and www.studentaid.ed.gov. Most colleges and technical schools also provide detailed information about financial aid on their individual websites.

Searching for specific scholarships should not be ignored. The class of the student (such as race, gender, or sexual orientation), area of study, membership in certain organizations and other elements can lead to **specialized financial aid** options. An example of a resource in this arena is "The Higher Education Money Book for Women and Minorities" published by Young, Mathews & Cox.

A great resource for counselors is the financial aid workshops offered by many colleges and universities to interested high schools free of charge. It is the counselor's job to organize and advertise the workshop which is provided by college staff members who are experts in financial aid. Sponsoring a **Financial Aid Night** is an excellent way for students and parent/guardian(s) to gain useful information about aid options and build relationships with the counselors. It is also another chance for the school to promote the guidance program.

Local public and college libraries can be good sources of information as well. Further, it is important that the counselor attends workshops explaining the new regulations involving federal money sources such as the *Pell Grant* and other federal funding sources for educational loans.

COMPETENCY 7.0   SUMMARY

Learning Styles: Counselors need to be familiar with different learning styles. This includes different levels of tolerance for noise, light, temperature, as well as different motivational levels. Instructional adjustments need to be made for different motivational levels and learning problems.

Learning style inventories such as the Dunn & Dunn Learning Style Inventory might be useful in determining students' styles.

Post-secondary Education: Counselors must be knowledgeable about the different options for postsecondary education, which include community college, four-year colleges, vocational training, and training offered by the military. Students considering the military will need to take the ASVAB (Armed Services Vocational Aptitude Battery) test.

Educational and Vocational Information Sources: Accurate, up-to-date information can be located through computer-based programs such as Discover, or through guides published by Barron and Petersons. Various resources are available online and in local libraries. Two free non-commercial websites with good information are www.finaid.org and www.studentaid.ed.gov.

Providing Educational and Vocational Information: Counselors should begin discussing general plans for postsecondary education at the beginning of high school, since this will impact course selection.

Counselors are expected to be able to direct families to reliable sources of information on scholarships and financial aid. They may want to coordinate a Financial Aid Night to be presented by experts from local colleges.

COMPETENCY 8.0 KNOWLEDGE OF RESEARCH, EVALUATION, AND FOLLOW-UP

Practicing counselors most appropriately engage in research addressing day to day encounters of helping students with behavior change. Often the problem needs to be one that can be experimented with in the school setting to attain these ends. Sometimes a staff member, in discussion with the counselor will mention a need to have more information in a certain area. In that case the counselor can count on the cooperation of that staff member for use of their students in the research project. Occasionally, counselors collaborate with researchers from local colleges or agencies.

SKILL 8.1 Purposes, Types and Basic Steps in Research, Evaluation and Follow-Up

Purposes of Research

1. Basic Research - This is the type of research done for knowledge without a stated practical application. It is often the result of a professional researcher's desire to obtain more knowledge about certain phenomena and is usually done in a clinical or scientific laboratory setting. Application of the results is not considered.

2. Applied Research - The techniques used in applied research are the same as those used in basic research. The purpose of the research is in applying the results to the improvement of methods of delivering education to enhance the learning process.

3. Action Research - This is the type of research that is directed at a specific problem to be solved. It is done with the immediate goal of applying the results to that specific problem and not done to develop a theory or to create generalizations.

Types of Research

1. Historical Research - This type of research is designed to apply the scientific method to describing and analyzing the past, in order to understand the present and perhaps predict the future.

2. Descriptive Research - In this work, analysis of the relationships between non-controllable variables and the development of generalizations based on these non-controllable variables is the goal. The formation of generalizations, often used in educational research, can lead to false results as the variables cannot be controlled, human subjects cannot be utilized, and the causes of the problem are often more complicated than the result of a single variable.

a. Assessment - Is the description given to such types of studies as surveys, polls, activity analysis, and trends. No value judgments, explanation of reasons or causes, or recommendations are given.

b. Evaluation - Is the value judgment with regard to the effectiveness, desirability or utility of a research project. Some examples of evaluation studies are school surveys (e.g., the student use of drugs) and follow-up studies. Application of findings to solving the particular problem is included in the study without any attempt to generalize.

3. Experimental and Quasi-Experimental Research - Is a logical and systematic way of answering the question "If this is done under carefully controlled conditions, what will happen?" This type of research is complicated and does not lend itself easily to the counselor using it in a school setting.

4. Single Subject Experimental Research - This type of research focuses upon the individual and not on the results of group experimentation. It is used to test hypotheses of the effect of a particular treatment on one or more behaviors or phenomena.

5. Qualitative Research - Focuses upon in-depth interviews, observations, and document analysis. Methods used in this type of holistic educational research include document and content analysis, case studies, and cultural anthropology. This type of research interprets data without the use of numerical analysis.

Basic Steps in Research - All research is based upon the use of the scientific method. This is the attempt to control as many variables of a problem as possible in order to separate out the influences of individual and specific elements of the problem.

1. Selecting the Research Problem - The practicing counselor usually has no problem selecting a problem that needs to be solved in the setting in which their work is conducted. The main consideration in the selection of the research problem is determining what can actually be studied. That is, can this variable be observed and measured? Is there an instrument available to measure this variable? If not, can one be designed?

2. Develop the Research Problem - The importance of this step in research cannot be too strongly emphasized. Research cannot be conducted on a problem that has not been fully developed. Various parts of the problem should be defined with the help of those familiar with the problem, talking about the problem with colleagues, and thinking about all the aspects of the problem.

Factors, variables and assumptions about the problem that will have an impact on the outcome of the problem should be identified. These variables are an integral part of the research project.

Review of the literature is one of the more important ongoing activities in which the researcher can engage. The reference part of the library contains many sources of information besides scholarly works, to acquaint oneself with what the public feels is important. Incorporating public interest in the project gives the work added benefit.

3. Formulate the Research Question - This statement includes all aspects of the question the researcher seeks to answer. It is specific in defining the population involved, gives a general description of the situation under which the research will be conducted, and always states the comparison group or groups to be compared. I is posed in the form of a question.

    a. Purpose statement - This statement tells what the study intends to do and how it will aid the researcher in answering the question(s) posed. In proposals, this statement is written in the present tense; in completed research this statement is written in the past tense.

    b. Procedural statement - This statement follows naturally from the purpose statement. It tells the reader what actions were taken to gain the results of the study.

    c. Hypotheses - This is the statement of what the researcher believes will be the relationship between the variables. The *research hypothesis* is what the researcher believes will be found as a result of the research. The *null hypothesis* is the statistical and logical opposite of the research hypothesis. Since we cannot often predict what will happen, we can often predict what will not happen. This is the purpose of the null hypotheses. The *alternative hypothesis* is a statement of the possibility of other variables not specifically addressed in the design.

4. Organize the Plan for the Research Report - The research report has the following components.

a. Introduction
b. Hypotheses
c. Review of the literature
d. Method, or research design, used in conducting the research
e. Results
f. Conclusions
g. Discussion
h. References

Basic Steps in Evaluation and Follow-Up

The evaluation of the research should be done by an unbiased party due to the critical nature of the evaluation. Some of the following questions should be asked in the critique. Does the title of the research clearly reflect the research done? Is the problem and hypothesis clearly defined and testable? Are terms defined? Is the related literature summarized adequately, relative to the problem, is it well organized, and are important findings emphasized? Is the design described adequately, are variables and samples described, are controls and data gathering instruments and procedures appropriate, and can the research be replicated? Do the results of the research use appropriate statistics, tables, and charts, and is the analysis of the relationship of the data logical and objective? Finally, is the discussion of the research clear and objective, and are the findings justified by the data presented?

The follow-up procedure is done after the program has been in effect for an established period of time. Longitudinal studies can be done to see if the program established by the research is still effective after a period of time; a survey instrument can be used in follow-up studies to ascertain if the participants felt there was a significant change from before the study, and to see if the results of the program established from the research study are relatively permanent in nature.

SKILL 8.2 Needs Assessment and Program Evaluation Techniques

Needs Assessment - The needs assessment is an extensive preliminary study of the real and perceived wants and requirements of a population, community or group. A series of complete and extensive questions are formulated to be submitted to all facets of the population involved. As an example, a needs assessment of a school community would consist of community taxpayers, community leaders, parents, school administrators, teachers, support staff and students. Other individuals may come forward who wish to participate in the study and they should be included if they have a connection with the purpose of the study. The design of the needs assessment study should be carefully formulated so the results can be analyzed in relation to the purpose of the study.

Program Evaluation Techniques - Program evaluation is often a requirement of funding sources or of administrators. Some there is a sincere wish to see if a program is producing the desired results; other times the demand for an evaluation is the result of political pressure, to either discredit opponents of the program or to strengthen their own positions on the value of the program. Finances influence the requirement of a program evaluation for a variety of reasons.

There are two broad types of evaluation: formative and summative.

Formative Evaluation - This type of evaluation involves the collection of data while a program is in the *developmental, implementational*, or *operational* stage. In the *developmental* stage the evaluator tries to determine the general goals, the specific outcomes or behaviors to be attained, and the current performance level of the population of the program to be evaluated. In the *implementational* stage the evaluator tries to determine if the program is implemented appropriately and the identified population is participating in the program. In the *operational* stage the evaluator looks at how well the program is running. Other information to gather is finding out if the staff is adequate and well trained and if any unanticipated difficulties have surfaced.

Summative Evaluation - This type of evaluation involves the collection of data after a program has been in place for a period of time. The summative evaluation is often done after one year of operation. This may not be an adequate amount of time to determine the effectiveness of the program, depending on the nature of the program. The summative evaluation often is used to determine if the program will be continued.

Models used in evaluation can be classified in the following manner.

The **CIPP Model** has four stages. *Context evaluation* identifies the elements of a setting and the discrepancies between what exists and what is desirable. *Input evaluation* is the analysis of available resources and methods for the selection of the most appropriate course of action. *Process evaluation* is the collection of data about the progress of the program. *Product evaluation* is the process of determining the extent to which the program has achieved its goals. In this model the evaluator gathers the information needed to make a decision in each stage and presents this material to the administrator for decision making.

Discrepancy Evaluation - The evaluator compares the degree of agreement between program standards and program performance. *Program standards* are the criteria the developers of the program identified for utilization of resources, procedural operations, program management and final outcomes. *Program performance* is what actually occurred when the program was operational in the educational setting. The five questions the evaluator answers are:

> Are standards defined in measurable terms?
> Are behavioral objectives stated clearly?
> What instruments are developed or selected to measure the standards?
> What data has been collected on performance?
> Has the data been used to determine the discrepancy between standards and performance?

The findings of the evaluator are then submitted in a report.

Adversarial Evaluation - The evaluator and administrator, with the help of the personnel involved in the program, compile a list of issues to evaluate. Issues are selected that are determined to be the most important to the success of the program. Selected personnel form teams to either support or oppose the program, gathering information to support their stand and prepare arguments for their side of the issues. The teams present their arguments before a panel of decision makers who make the final decision as to the modification, elimination or retention of the program.

SKILL 8.3 Interpretation of Results of Research, Evaluation and Follow-Up

In the discussion portion of the research project, the level of significance of the study is reported by the researcher. This is most often used in determining the effectiveness of the research with evaluation and follow-up of the procedures used. The attainment of statistical significance (usually reported as 0.05 level of significance, meaning the results were unlikely to be attained by chance) is not always the determining factor of the worth of a program. The evaluator of the program must interpret what the results mean, the influence of the variables on those results and the relation of each statistical analysis to the hypothesis formulated at the beginning of the study.

Practical significance is another criterion for judging the contribution of the study to every day practice. Implications for possible change derived from the practical application of the results may be valuable for the improvement of the program. Shortcomings in the research may become evident by the results and therefore additional studies and research should be considered.

SKILL 8.4 Developing Objectives and Determining Outcomes Based on Data

New and innovative programs and methods are sometimes introduced without careful consideration of their value for the setting in which they are to be used. The school counselor should assess new programs before implementing them.

Factors to consider are:

- Will this program be acceptable to the community?
- What will be the cost to the school district?
- Can grant money be obtained to initiate the program?
- Will that money be available on a continuous basis or will it run out after a period of time?

A needs assessment of the school community might be in order to see if the program is acceptable. As an example, the health department might feel a program of smoking cessation would be beneficial to the students. In a needs assessment survey, students might feel that smoking is a desired activity on their part and so they would not attend this type of activity. It might be more advantageous to the health department to develop a unit on the health damage smoking causes to the individual in later life.

Before adding a program to the guidance and counseling curriculum, how this task will be accomplished should be evaluated. Will new staff be needed or will this program fall to the existing staff? If the latter is the case, will other programs now in existence have less time allotted or can some ineffective program now be eliminated? Can the staff view the suggested new program in operation in another school? If this can be done, the counselors in the other school should be questioned as to the strengths and weaknesses of the program, how they would change the program, and what benefits have the students experienced by instituting this program.

Program objectives should be developed before the adoption of any program. These objectives are based upon the needs of the population to be served and can be drawn from the needs assessment. Program objectives should be written with measurable goals and a clear methodology for evaluating the achievement or lack of achievement of the goals.

After all evaluative data have been compiled and analyzed, the person in charge of the program determines the degree to which program objectives have been obtained. If the formulation of the program objectives was done carefully and there is indisputable evidence that these objectives have not been reached, it is ethical to eliminate the program and start again from scratch. If there is an undeniable opinion that the program objectives have been obtained, then the retention of the program and further plans for expansion should be the result.

Problems can arise when there is no clear evidence of attainment of program objectives, or if some of the objectives have been attained but others, considered more important, have not been accomplished. It is clear that modification of the program is in order. The task of rebuilding the methods in order to reach the stated objectives should begin with a new perspective of what needs to be done to improve the program. Perhaps people who have not had initial input into the program should be recruited to help in the revision of the program. Perhaps the original objectives of the program were unrealistic. These can be difficult questions to resolve and require thought and effort.

COMPETENCY 8.0   SUMMARY

Basic Research: This is the type of research done for knowledge without a stated practical application.

Applied Research: The purpose of the research is in applying the results to the improvement of methods of delivering education to enhance the learning process or some other desired end.

Action Research: This is the type of research that is done to immediately apply the results to that specific problem and not done to develop a theory or for creating generalizations.

Assessment: These are studies such as surveys, polls, activity analysis, and trends.

Qualitative Research: This work focuses upon in-depth interviews, observations, and document analysis (in contrast with quantitative research, which deals mainly with numbers)

Literature Review: A review of the literature involves reviewing all the prior research on the subject.

Research follows the scientific method: Define the question; Gather information and resources; Form hypothesis; Perform experiment and collect data; Analyze data; Interpret data and draw conclusions ; Publish results

Program Evaluation: In school settings, counselors are increasingly being asked to engage in "program evaluation" to determine if funded programs are producing desired results. This involves collecting objective and reliable data. Some data are *formative* (collected during the process of developing a program)and others are *summative* (collected at the end of the program). Different models of evaluation include CIPP, Discrepancy Evaluation and Adversarial Evaluation.

Statistical significance: The baseline for statistical significance is typically reported at the .05 level, which means it is 95% unlikely that the results were obtained by chance.

COMPETENCY 9.0 KNOWLEDGE OF CURRENT TRENDS & TECHNIQUES

SKILL 9.1 Prevention and Positive School Environments

In addition to providing counseling after a problem has been identified, it is the task of the school counselor to contribute to the school's effort to prevent difficulties before they arise. Helping to create a positive school environment is a major part of any prevention effort. Other elements of prevention have been discussed previously, such as the importance of attending to issues of bullying, prejudice, aggression and violence in the school setting. Further, teaching communication, self-awareness and conflict resolution skills to students are also effective prevention approaches, as noted earlier.

Creating Positive School Environments

A fundamental task of all schools today is creating a positive environment within which all students are respected and can thrive. The school counselor can be instrumental in facilitating the positive school environment. While this task cannot be achieved alone by the school counselor or the guidance department, counselors need to be alert to the ways in which positive school environments can be established.

Positive school environments share these qualities:

- Core values of respect, integrity, cooperation and care for one another.

- Adults strive to be caring, competent and "in charge" without abusing their power and authority.

- Clear and direct communication is valued, practiced and taught.

- Student success is measured not only by academic achievement but also by the physical, mental, social and emotional health of students.

- Avoidance of stereotyping and bias while still acknowledging and valuing diversity.

- An attitude of "we are all in this together" rather than an "us vs. them" mentality, including a sense of partnership with parent/guardians and the community.

- Opportunities for students to get to know and work with students who are different from them.

- Refusal to allow sexual and other forms of harassment and bullying.

- Conflict resolution, problem-solving skills and violence prevention programs built into the curriculum.

- Policies and procedures are proactive and preventive in nature, including but not limited to crisis management planning and the creation of a safe school climate.

These qualities should exist across the entire school community. In positive school environments, the values and characteristics described above are present among the student population, among the staff, faculty and administration, and between the students and the adults in the school. Ideally, these qualities are also present at the school board level and in all interactions with parents/guardians and community members.

Basic Prevention Concepts

Some key prevention concepts include the following ideas:

Maintain an open door policy. Students need to know that the school counselor is there to help. An attitude of openness and positive communication can encourage students to seek assistance when something concerns them before it escalates into a larger problem.

Create a student assistance team (SAP). By designating and training a group of teachers and staff (counselors, psychologist, nurse, social worker, etc.) as people students can go to when they are experiencing difficulties, the school offers students the opportunity to get the help they need to be successful in school. SAPs provide early intervention and referral, and have the advantage of being interdisciplinary and collaborative.

Implement programs that involve students in the school community in innovative ways. By engaging students in programs beyond the scope of the classroom and traditional guidance functions, they become invested in the larger school community. This enhances their self-esteem and helps forge new bonds among students. At times, peers are able to help students when adults are less able to do so. Attention needs to be given to recruitment of students for such programs, and adequate orientation, training and supervision must be provided.

Such programs might include the following:

1. **Cross-age teaching:** Have high school students help with programs for elementary and middle school students. These could involve tutoring, conflict resolution, peer mediation, or orientation for students moving from one school building to the next.

2. **New student welcoming committee:** Establish a group of students who are willing to mentor students new to the district. They can sit with their mentees at lunch and share information about the school. New friendships may develop, and both mentors and mentees have the chance to meet people who are perhaps different from them.

3. **Service clubs:** Sponsor or help start a service club oriented to helping students implement projects that improve the school and community environment. Some examples are a recycling project within the school, a holiday gift program for needy families, and a volunteer program to help the elderly in the community or to bring seasonal artwork to nursing home patients.

Student involvement in the guidance program: Inviting students to help out with guidance activities such as Career Day or Financial Aid Night or with office tasks can be worthwhile to students who are interested.

SKILL 9.2   Crisis Management

Crisis and emergency situations are events beyond the realm of every day life. They always involve some degree of surprise, shock, loss and emotion. Crises include death, natural disasters such as earthquakes and hurricanes, vehicular and other accidents, school shootings, and other forms of extreme violence. The unpredictability of crises, the experience of loss that invariably accompanies such situations and the strong feelings that are evoked all make crisis and emergency events particularly potent and challenging for everyone involved.

The value of being prepared

Pre-planning and training in basic crisis management skills can be extremely helpful in responding effectively. Although the events themselves may be unpredictable, there is a body of information about how people react to crisis and what responders can do to ameliorate and manage the aftermath of crisis. This is important in school settings, where there are a large number of people congregated in one place and contagion is a concern. Anxiety and misinformation can spread like wildfire, exacerbating the short and long term effects of traumatic events.

Designating and training a crisis response team can be quite beneficial. Comprehensive crisis management training as well as ongoing refresher courses are necessary for a team to function well. In most cases, the school counselor is integrally involved in the work of crisis team. He or she may be a leader or not, depending on the structure of the team, the preferences of the administration, and the background of the counselor.

In addition to a crisis team, school districts need to have clearly defined crisis response plans. They should include as much detail as possible, with specific recommendations for different situations as needed, although a general plan is applicable in many circumstances. The plan should incorporate the following:

- delineate the school's goals in crisis situations (such as maintaining as normal a school day as possible, or providing timely information),
- identify key players on the crisis response team,
- specify how communication will be handled,
- describe what interventions will be used with students,
- note how interactions and referrals to outside agencies will be managed, and
- detail what follow-up is needed.

Further, it helps to have handouts about traumatic stress reactions, sample letters to parents and guardians, press releases (when necessary) and other useful documents ready prior to any event.

The need for information

Everyone who experiences a traumatic event needs to be aware of the normal reactions and common feelings of survivors, as well as receive accurate information about the event itself (when this is not known) and what the school is doing in response. This means that the district needs to make clear decisions about the actions the school is taking, including what parents and guardians need to know and do, and communicate these plans succinctly and in a timely manner to all in the school community. Information also needs to flow to the larger community. Specific, to-the-point information is valuable; avoid all rumors.

Intervention for students

Most commonly, school counselors and other school personnel will be available for crisis counseling and support in a designated room for a day or two after a traumatic event. Some districts will invite local experts in traumatic stress response or grief counseling to come to the school to aid school personnel. Interventions include listening, normalizing the reactions of students, offering to call parents and guardians, and making arrangements for the student to go home early when needed. Referrals to outside professionals may also be made.

TEACHER CERTIFICATION STUDY GUIDE

Self-care during and after the event

Part of a school crisis plan should spell out how responders and other school personnel will receive and give support during the implementation of the crisis management plan. Further, school counselors and other personnel need to get rest and support after doing crisis response work. This work is very demanding and the effects on responders may not be immediately apparent. Secondary post-traumatic stress is a concern, particularly when the crisis response team has multiple or ongoing situations to manage. Adequate administrative and personal support, time off, and sufficient training and de-briefing are essential.

The following websites have information about school crisis management, traumatic stress reactions, and related topics:

www.nctsnet.org/nccts/nav.do?pid=ctr_aud_schlmeans that part of the crisis response
 www.cdc.gov/niosh/unp-trinstrs.html
 www.aaets.org/trresp.htm
www.apa.org/practice/traumaticstress.html
www.ed.gov/admins/lead/safety/training/responding/crisis_pg11.html?exp=2.

SKILL 9.3   Using Technology Effectively

The core of a school counselor's job involves communication and connection with students, parents/guardians, teachers, administrators, other school personnel and outside professionals. The personal relationship between counselors and others cannot be supplanted by technology. However, since communication and information are central to a school counselor's work, technology can be utilized very effectively to enhance the school counselor's functioning.

There are several areas in which school counselors need to be technologically proficient. One is in basic computer skills, such as keyboarding, word processing, and using email. Many schools have computerized much student data and scheduling, and therefore school counselors must be able to access and utilize this information efficiently. Email is also a primary form of communication in many school districts, and counselors, like all faculty and staff, must be able to communicate using this format.

Increasingly, parents and guardians are also using email to communicate with school personnel. Some school districts have created specific interactive programs on the school's website to facilitate the sharing of information with parents, guardians, community members, teachers and other school personnel.

A second area in which school counselors are increasingly required to be technologically savvy is in the use of the internet to access information. While there are many types of internet information that may be relevant to school counselors' work, of particular importance is information about career development, higher education, training programs, and financial aid. Students and many parents/guardians utilize the internet as their primary source for gathering data, and counselors must be able to interact intelligently with and even guide students in their search for information. This requires not only a facility in using internet browsers and search engines, but the capacity to assess the value and utility of different websites.

Thirdly, counselors need to be able to use software to develop presentations and graphics for the classroom, at conferences or meetings, for reports, and with colleagues. Most professional fields require such capacity and school counselors need to stay current with the opportunities offered by technology. This may also involve a working knowledge of hardware used for presentations.

BIBLIOGRAPHY

BEST, J.W. & KAHN, J.V., (1996), *Research in Education,* 7th Edition. Boston: Allyn & Bacon, Inc.

BRAGSTAD, B.J., & STUMPF, S. M., (1987), *A Guidebook for Teaching Study Skills and Motivation,* 2nd Edition, Boston: Allyn & Bacon, Inc.

BROWNELL, J., (1986), *Building Active Listening Skills,* Englewood Cliffs, NJ: Prentice-Hall Inc.

BUKSTEIN, O.G., (1995), *Substance Abuse - Adolescent Assessment & Prevention,* John Wiley & Sons.

BURLEY-ALLEN, M., (1982), *Listening: The Forgotten Skill,* Hoboken, NJ: John Wiley & Sons, Inc.

CARTWRIGNT, D., & ZANDER, A., Editors, (1968), *Group Dynamics, Research & Theory,* 3rd Edition, New York: Harper & Row.

CATES, W.M., (1985), *A Practical Guide to Educational Research,* Englewood Cliffs, NJ: Prentice-Hall Inc.

COREY, G., (1991), *Manual For Theory & Practice of Counseling & Psychotherapy,* 4th Edition, Pacific Grove, CA: Brooks/Cole Publishing Co.

COREY, G., (1996), *Instructor's Manual for Theory & Practice of Counseling & Psychotherapy,* 5th Edition, Pacific Grove, CA: Brooks/Cole Publishing Co.

COREY, G., (1996), *Student Manual for Theory & Practice of Counseling & Psychotherapy,* 5th Edition, Pacific Grove, CA:, Brooks/Cole Publishing Co.

COREY, G., (1990), *Theory & Practice of Group Counseling,* 3rd Edition, Pacific Grove, CA: Brooks/Cole Publishing Co.

COTTLE, W.C., (1968), *Guidance Monograph Series, Series 111, Testing, Interest & Personality Inventories,* Boston: Houghton Mifflin Co.

DOUGHERTY, A.M., (1995), *Case Studies in Human Services Consultation,* Pacific Grove, CA: Brooks/Cole Publishing Co.

DOWNING, L.N., (1968), *Guidance & Counseling Services, An Introduction,* New York, McGraw-Hill Book Co.

DRESHMAN, J.L., CRABBE, C.L. & TARASEVICH, S. (2001), *Caring in Times of Crisis: A Crisis Management/Postvention Manual for Administrators, Student Assistance Teams & Other School Personnel K-12.* Chapin, SC: Youthlight, Inc.

DUNN, R. & DUNN, K., (1978), *Teaching Students through Their Individual Learning Styles, A Practical Approach,* Reston, VA: Reston Publishing Co.

ERIKSON, E.H., (1963), *Childhood & Society,* 2nd Edition, New York, W.W. Norton & Co. Inc.

Florida School Laws, Florida Statues, 1996 Edition, Chapters 228-246.

Florida School Code, 1994 Edition, Chapters 228-246.

GOLDMAN, L., (1961), *Century Psychology Series, Using Tests in Counseling,* New York, Appleton-Century Crofts.

GRESSARD, C.F., & KEEL, L. *Counseling Today,* February 1998, *Ethics in Counseling,* pg. 16.

GUERNSEY, T.F. & KLARE, K., (1993), *Special Education Law,* Durham, NC: Carolina Academic Press.

HAZLER, R.J., PH.D., (1996), *Breaking the Cycle of Violence,* Washington, DC: Accelerated Development.

HERGENHAHN B.R., (1988), *An Introduction to Theories of Learning,* 3rd Edition, Englewood Cliffs, NJ: Prentice-Hall Inc.

JOHNSON, D.W., JOHNSON, R.T., (1995), *Reducing School Violence through Conflict Resolution,* Alexandria, VA: Association for Supervision & Curriculum Development.

JOHNSON, D.W., & JOHNSON, F.P., (1975), *Joining Together, Group Theory & Group Skills,* Englewood Cliffs, NJ: Prentice-Hall Inc.

KEMP, C.G., (1964), *Perspectives on the Group Process,* Boston, Houghton Mifflin Co.

LYMAN, H.B., (1968), *Guidance Monograph Series, Series 111 Testing, Intelligence, Aptitude & Achievement Testing,* Boston: Houghton Mifflin Co.

MAHLER, C., CALDWELL, E., (1961), *Group Counseling in Secondary Schools,* Chicago, IL: Science Research Associates.

MAHLER, C., (1969). *Group Counseling in the School.* Boston: Houghton Mifflin Co.

MEYERING R.A., (1968), *Guidance Monograph Series,, Series 11 Counseling, Use of Test Data in Counseling,* Boston: Houghton Mifflin Co.

MCDANIELS, C., NORMAN, C.G., (1992), *Counseling for Career Development,* 1st Edition, San Francisco: Jossey-Bass Publishers.

Forum Guide to the Privacy of Student Information: A Resource for Schools (NFES 2006–805). (2006). U.S. Dept of Education. Washington, DC: National Center for Education Statistics.

OSIPOW, S.H., (1968), *Theories of Career Development,* New York, Century Psychology Series, Appleton-Century Crofts, Educational Division of Meredith Corp.

OSIPOW, S.H., FITZGERALD, L.F., (1996), *Theories of Career Development,* 4th Edition, Boston: Allyn & Bacon.

OSIPOW, S.H., & WALSH, W.B., (1970), *Strategies in Counseling for Behavior Change,* New York: Century Psychology Series, Appleton-Century Crofts.

PATTERSON, C.H., (1966), *Theories of Counseling & Psychotherapy,* New York, Harper-Row.

REEVES, E.T., (1970), *The Dynamics of Group Behavior,* New York: American Management Association, Inc.

ROGERS, D., (1969), *Readings in Child Psychology,* Pacific Groves, CA: Brooks/Cole Publishing Co.

SHAW, M.E., (1976), *Group Dynamics - The Psychology of Small Group Behavior,* 2nd Edition, New York: McGraw-Hill Book Co.

SIMS, R.R., & SIMS, S.J., (1995), *The Importance of Learning Styles,* Westport, CT: Greenwood Press.

VANDRACEK, R.M., LERNER, M.R., & SCHULENBERG, J.E., (1986), *Career Development: A Life Span Developmental Approach,* Hillsdale, NJ: Lawrence Erlbaum Associates.

TOUYZ, S.W., & BEUMONT, P.J.V., Editors, (1985), *Eating Disorders, Prevalence & Treatment,* Williams & Wilkend - ADIS-TTY, Limited.

WHITE, J., MULLIS, F., EARLEG, B., & BRIGMAN, G., (1995), *Consultation in Schools, The Counselors Role,* Portland, ME: J. Weston Walch.

ZEBROWITZ, L.A., (1990), *Social Perception,* Pacific Grove, CA: Brooks/Cole Publishers.

ZUNKER, V.G., (1994), *Using Assessment Results for Career Development,* 4th Edition. Pacific Grove, CA: Brooks/Cole Publishers.

Sample Test

Directions: Read each item and select the best response.

1. **Present behavior is a result of early childhood experiences, the unconscious, and the incomplete attainment of a stage in psychosexual development.**
   (Average Rigor) (Skill 1.1)

   A. Gestalt

   B. Existential Therapy

   C. Psychoanalytic Therapy

   D. Person-Centered Therapy

2. **A technique used in this therapy is the completion of a life-style assessment.**
   (Rigorous) (Skill 1.1)

   A. Existential Therapy

   B. Alderian Therapy

   C. Behavior Therapy

   D. Reality Therapy

3. **The thinking through of irrational thoughts that have resulted in emotional problems is the basis of this theory**
   (Rigorous) (Skill 1.1)

   A. Reality Therapy

   B. Gestalt Therapy

   C. Behavior Therapy

   D. Rational Emotive Behavior Therapy

4. **Dreams are analyzed by having the client describe their feelings as they act out all parts of the dream**
   (Average Rigor) (Skill 1.1)

   A. Gestalt Therapy

   B. Psychoanalytic Therapy

   C. Behavior Therapy

   D. Person-Centered Therapy

5. In psychoanalytic therapy the technique not used is:
   (Rigorous) (Skill 1.1)

   A. Dream Analysis

   B. Interpretation

   C. Free Association

   D. The ABC approach

6. Unconscious processes that shield the individual from threatening and anxiety-producing thoughts are all of the following except:
   (Rigorous) (Skill 1.1)

   A. Rationalizations

   B. Resistance

   C. Ego-Defense Mechanisms

   D. Sublimation

7. The process of an active organism exhibiting controlled behavior is called:
   (Average Rigor) (Skill 1.1)

   A. Operant Conditioning

   B. Modeling

   C. Counterconditioning

   D. Transference

8. Questions of freedom, choice and responsibility are addressed in:
   (Average Rigor) (Skill 1.1)

   A. Reality Theory

   B. Existentialism Theory

   C. Behavior Theory

   D. Person-Centered Theory

9. The ability to be true to our ideas of a meaningful life and accept responsibility for the choices we make is called:
   (Average Rigor) (Skill 1.1)

   A. Phenomenology

   B. Authenticity

   C. Restricted Existence

   D. Denial

10. The therapist, in person-centered therapy, should have all the following personality characteristics except:
    (Average Rigor) (Skill 1.1)

    A. Genuineness

    B. Unconditional Positive Regard

    C. Empathic Understanding

    D. Polarized Thinking

11. The layers of neurosis in Perl's Gestalt theory are all the following except:
    (Rigorous) (Skill 1.1)

    A. Phobic Layer

    B. Impasse Layer

    C. Meaninglessness layer

    D. Explosive Layer

12. Turning back to ourselves things we would like to do or have done to others is called:
    (Average Rigor) (Skill 1.1)

    A. Retroflection

    B. Introjection

    C. Deflection

    D. Confluence

13. The psychological needs in reality theory are all of the following except:
    (Easy) (Skill 1.1)

    A. Fun

    B. Power

    C. Belonging

    D. Success

14. The WDEP model in reality theory includes all the following except:
    (Rigorous) (Skill 1.1)

    A. Wants

    B. Direction

    C. Evaluation

    D. Planning and Commitment

15. In cognitive behavior therapy the multimodal therapy was originated by:
    (Rigorous) (Skill 1.1)

    A. Albert Ellis

    B. Carl Rogers

    C. Arnold Lazarus

    D. Margaret Mahler

16. The stages of life in Erik Erikson's psychosocial theory include all of the following except:
    (Rigorous) (Skill 1.1)

    A. Innocence vs. Generativity

    B. Basic Trust vs. Basic Mistrust

    C. Identity vs. Role Confusion

    D. Ego Integrity vs. Despair

17. Stages of human development as outlined by Jean Piaget include all of the following except:
    (Average Rigor) (Skill 1.2)

    A. Sensormotor Stage

    B. Concrete Operational Stage

    C. Cultural and Environmental Stage

    D. Formal Operational Stage

18. With regard to counseling, it is beyond the scope of the school counselor's role to:
    (Average Rigor) (Skill 1.4)

    A. Provide individual and group counseling

    B. Provide crisis intervention

    C. Provide family consultation

    D. Provide mental health evaluations

19. Categories of theories of learning are all the following except:
    (Rigorous) (Skill 1.2)

    A. Behavioristic

    B. Functionalistic

    C. Associationistic

    D. Cognitive

20. In applying counseling theories to specific situations it is important that the counselor does all of the following except:
    (Average Rigor) (Skill 1.3)

    A. Create a rapport with the student

    B. Pick a theory to apply and stick to that theory.

    C. Involve the student in the decision making process

    D. Encourage the student to make his/her own decisions.

21. **A disadvantage of group counseling is:**
    (Rigorous) (Skill 1.4)

    A. The presence of a built in support system

    B. A non-threatening atmosphere

    C. The ability to substitute the group for the real world, permitting the client unlimited time to make adjustments

    D. The counselor can reach more clients

22. **Limitations of group counseling are all of the following except:**
    (Average Rigor) (Skill 1.4)

    A. There is pressure to accept group values without analyzing them

    B. The counselor has to deal with a diverse population

    C. People sometimes function poorly in groups

    D. Individuals in the group can justify their present status by reinforcement from the group

23. **Group dynamics include all the following except:**
    (Average Rigor) (Skill 1.5)

    A. A Political entity created by building on the organization and management of groups.

    B. The employment of specific techniques and concepts to keep the group vitalized

    C. A branch of knowledge concerned with groups and their interactions, and interactions with other groups and individuals

    D. A description of individual behavior

24. **Group dynamics is all the following except:**
    (Rigorous) (Skill 1.5)

    A. An emphasis on empirical research and theory

    B. A branch of knowledge concerned mainly with the way groups form

    C. The relationships of groups with observable phenomena

    D. The interrelationship of all social science disciplines

25. **Elements of good listening skills include all the following except:**
 (Easy) (Skill 1.6)

   A. Involving strong emotions in the process of listening

   B. Being genuinely interested in the speaker

   C. Remembering what has been said

   D. Permitting a speaker to express him/herself fully

26. **Barriers to good listening are all of the following except:**
 (Easy) (Skill 1.6)

   A. Impatience with the speaker

   B. Faking Attention

   C. Being a sounding board

   D. Forming an opinion about the value of what is to be said before it is said

27. **Good responding skills include all the following except:**
 (Easy) (Skill 1.6)

   A. Ability to show your feelings without inhibitions

   B. Reflecting the person's feelings

   C. Giving constructive feedback

   D. Maintaining eye contact

28. **The developmental concept not included in existential therapy is:**
 (Rigorous) (Skill 1.2)

   A. Capacity for self-awareness

   B. Acceptance of responsibility for freedom

   C. Ability to direct one's life without therapeutic help

   D. Acceptance of the significance of death to the living

29. **A developmental concept not used in counseling theory is:**
    (Rigorous) (Skill 1.2)

    A. The behavior therapy concept of changing behavior based on present situations

    B. Freud's division of development into five stages

    C. The correction of irrational and illogical thinking are developmental tasks in REBT

    D. Learning ways to rationalize our behavior

30. **Effective study skills do not include:**
    (Easy) (Skill 1.8)

    A. Learning the material and then putting it aside until there is an exam scheduled

    B. Studying every day at a certain time

    C. Taking good notes

    D. Reviewing frequently

31. **All of the following are signs of anorexia nervosa except:**
    (Average Rigor) (Skill 1.7)

    A. Malnutrition

    B. Behavior regression

    C. No outward signs

    D. Recognizable weight loss

32. **Violence prevention programs do not include:**
    (Rigorous) (Skill 1.7)

    A. Conflict resolution seminars

    B. Behavior modification programs

    C. Training faculty and staff to intervene before violent confrontations occur

    D. Instituting a boxing program to train students to protect themselves

33. Effects of stereotyping and prejudice on victims do not include:
    (Rigorous) (Skill 1.7)

    A. Confrontation of the perpetrator by the victim

    B. The development of a sense of inferiority

    C. The development of a persecution complex

    D. Harboring of thoughts of violence toward the perpetrator

34. In helping students to make decisions, steps in the process do not include:
    (Average Rigor) (Skill 1.8)

    A. Defining the problem

    B. Listing all the options

    C. Surveying family, friends, and peers

    D. Making an informed decision based on the steps in the decision making process

35. Topics for discussion in the initial interview with a student to gain rapport do not include:
    (Rigorous) (Skill 1.9)

    A. Academic progress

    B. Activities in which the student is participating

    C. Difficulties in school adjustment for the entering student

    D. Matters of discipline referral

36. Ways not to be effective in communicating information to students are:
    (Easy) (Skill 1.9)

    A. Through individual interviews

    B. Through contacting friends and parents

    C. Through home room visitations

    D. Through monthly newsletters home

37. **Some current sources of professional information for counselors do not include:**
    (Easy) (Skill 1.10)

    A. Professional journals

    B. Workshops and conventions

    C. Visitations to other school programs

    D. Teenage magazines

38. **Advantages of holding a college night include all the following except:**
    (Average Rigor) (Skill 1.10)

    A. For counselors to be able to meet with their colleagues

    B. To bring a variety of post-secondary institutions together for the benefit of students and parents

    C. To initiate students into the college/post secondary admissions scene

    D. For counselors to get to know college admissions personnel

39. **The inaccuracy of test results caused by chance is called:**
    (Rigorous) (Skill 2.1)

    A. Standardization

    B. Standard Error of Measurement

    C. Standard Score

    D. Derived Score

40. **A statistical concept that measures the relationship between two factors in test validity is:**
    (Rigorous) (Skill 2.1)

    A. Reliability Coefficient

    B. Standard Deviation

    C. Raw Score

    D. Correlation Coefficient

41. **A condition that does not affect testing results is:**
    (Rigorous) (Skill 2.2)

    A. The physical and mental condition of the testee

    B. The testing room environment

    C. The colors of the clothes the proctors are wearing

    D. The validity of the test

42. All the following are advantages of testing except: *(Average Rigor) (Skill 2.3)*

   A. As a way to get multiple test interpretations

   B. As a way to help students recognize and use the resources they have

   C. As a way to present meaningful information to the student for decision making

   D. As a way to help identify options for the future

43. Disadvantages of testing are all the following except: *(Rigorous) (Skill2.3)*

   A. The possibility of results being used improperly

   B. The possibility of the student misinterpreting the test results

   C. The inherent subjectivity of tests administered for counseling purposes

   D. Using the test to predict future behavior

44. In the administration of tests, procedures should include all the following except: *(Rigorous) (Skill 2.4)*

   A. Safeguarding the tests

   B. Informing the students of the nature of the test by giving them questions from the test

   C. Guarding the tests in the exam room when students have access to the room

   D. Guarding the tests by not leaving them where students and non-authorized personnel have access

45. In interpreting test results the counselor should not: *(Average Rigor) (Skill 2.5)*

   A. Relate the results to the goals that had previously been determined

   B. Provide for individual interpretation

   C. Wait to interpret the tests when the student is scheduling the following year's courses

   D. Give the student input into the interpretation of the test results

46. **If tests need to be interpreted in a group the counselor should not:**
    (Average Rigor) (Skill 2.5)

    A. Announce individual test scores

    B. Explain the norm group to which the students have been compared

    C. Provide for private individual interpretation for students

    D. Explain statistics of the test so students can understand the meaning of their scores

47. **The written report of test results and interpretation should not:**
    (Average Rigor) (Skill 2.5)

    A. Be written in understandable language

    B. Always include charts and graphs

    C. Be disseminated on a need to know basis

    D. Be written in the language of testing

48. **In accurately reporting test results for interpretation by others all the following guidelines should be used except:**
    (Rigorous) (Skill 2.6)

    A. A uniform method of recording should be employed

    B. Consistency in language used should be employed

    C. The purpose, limitations, and the validity of the test should be stated

    D. The receiver of the results should be required to contact the counselor in order to receive the counselor's candid opinion

49. **In interpreting test results to other professionals and parents, the counselor does not always have to:**
    (Average Rigor) (Skill 2.7)

    A. Be thoroughly familiar with the test

    B. Let other staff members see the results of the test

    C. Notify the student that the counselor will be sharing the results with their parent/guardian(s)

    D. Work with the parents in a counseling relationship to help them understand their child's abilities

50. **In interpreting testing data from other professionals and testing firms, the counselor should do all the following except:**
(Average Rigor) (Skill 2.8)

   A. Understand the material in the report

   B. Go right to the summary and not worry about the technical aspects of the report

   C. Contact the writer of the report for clarification if needed

   D. Refer to the testing manual for clarification if needed

51. **The occupational environments of Holland's theory do not include:**
(Rigorous) (Skill 3.1)

   A. Artistic and social

   B. Realistic and conventional

   C. Enterprising and investigative

   D. Hostile and negative

52. **The classifications of career counseling theories do not include:**
(Rigorous) (Skill 3.1)

   A. Trait factor theory

   B. Developmental or self-concept theory

   C. No choice theory

   D. Personality and career choice theory

53. **Super's theory of vocations is based upon all of the following except:**
(Rigorous) (Skill 3.1)

   A. The inheritance of psychic energies

   B. The development of self-concepts

   C. External conditions that dictate the expression of self-concepts vocationally

   D. Developmental behavior theory

54. **Similarities in theories of vocational choice are all of the following except:**
    (Average Rigor) (Skill 3.1)

    A. They describe the relationship between two sets of observations

    B. They consider family influence on vocational choice a primary consideration

    C. They are usually based upon personality theory

    D. They emphasize the same types of critical periods in career development

55. **Shadowing is not:**
    (Easy) (Skill 3.2)

    A. Spending an extended period of time with a particular person in a chosen field

    B. A paid experience

    C. A learning experience by the student and the business volunteer

    D. Experiencing the daily routine of a particular business

56. **The purpose of a career day includes all of the following except:**
    (Average Rigor) (Skill 3.2)

    A. Make contacts in the community for future job placement for students

    B. Make students aware of the qualifications needed for particular jobs

    C. Give the students a break in the academic routine while giving them a valuable education experience

    D. Make available to students, in one place, occupational information for all levels of interests and abilities

57. **Computer generated career information systems do not include:**
    (Rigorous) (Skill 3.2)

    A. Choices

    B. GIS

    C. SIGI

    D. IDEA

58. Decision making occurs at all the following critical points in career development except:
    (Rigorous) (Skill 3.3)

    A. When a student enters high school

    B. In selecting an entry level job

    C. When selecting education plans

    D. In changing jobs

59. In the *anticipation* phase of decision making as outlined by Tiedman and O'Hara, the stages include all but:
    (Rigorous) (Skill 3.3)

    A. Exploration

    B. Crystallization

    C. Clarification

    D. Reevaluation

60. In Tiedman and O'Hara's *accommodation* phase of decision making, the stages include all but:
    (Rigorous) (Skill 3.3)

    A. Induction

    B. Initiation

    C. Reformation

    D. Integration

61. In evaluating education and career materials all the following should be considered except:
    (Average Rigor) (Skill 3.4)

    A. Appropriate vocabulary for the targeted age and reading level

    B. Verified accuracy of the information

    C. Material from advertisements and trade organizations

    D. The avoidance of the use of biased and stereotyping images

62. In evaluating content of career information, all the following areas should be included except:
    (Average Rigor) (Skill 3.4)

    A. The impressions of the reader as indicated by filling out an evaluation form

    B. The preparation required for entry level jobs

    C. The work setting and conditions of the career

    D. The long-term employment outlook

63. Methods of identifying materials to be used for career development include all of the following except:
(Average Rigor) (Skill 3.5)

   A. Read all material on the market and eliminate inappropriate material

   B. Acquire a good reference knowledge

   C. Monitor new information as it enters the system

   D. Have an organized system of reviewing material

64. Levels of career development can be divided into the following time periods
(Easy) (Skill 3.6)

   A. At the high school level

   B. At the college and young adult level

   C. At the time of marriage and children

   D. For older adults and those nearing retirement

65. The major steps in Zunker's 1994 model for using assessment results in developmental career counseling are:
(Rigorous) (Skill 3.6)

   A. Analyzing needs

   B. Establishing the purpose of the test

   C. Administering a complete battery of tests

   D. Utilizing the results of assessment

66. Some methods of teaching students to develop employability skills are:
(Rigorous) (Skill 3.7)

   A. Participation in a supervised job experience

   B. Write an essay about ways to get a job

   C. Award course credit for participation in a program of job preparation

   D. Have students interview potential employers to determine what they look for in employees

67. The role of the counselor in assisting students in exploring career and educational options includes all the following except:
   (Rigorous) (Skill 3.7)

   A. Have material for exploration[REC6] easily accessible

   B. Support and encourage students in their search for career choices

   C. Help students form realistic decisions

   D. Explain career choice theories to them

68. Sources of information on education and vocational choices include:
   (Average Rigor) (Skill 3.5)

   A. Neighbors and relatives

   B. American Trade School Directory

   C. The career guide of private schools *Getting Skilled, Getting Ahead*

   D. The local library

69. In evaluating the results of consultation, all the following factors should be considered except:
   (Rigorous) (Skill 4.1)

   A. The feelings of the student's parents as to the success of the process

   B. The report of the consultee as to the problem solving results

   C. An attitude change in the student

   D. Empirical results of an evaluation tool

70. Consultation process models include all the following except:
   (Average Rigor) (Skill 4.1)

   A. Doctor/patient model

   B. Friend of the family model

   C. Behavior consultation model

   D. Mental health consultation model

71. The settings in which consultation takes place can be all the following except:
    (Easy) (Skill 4.1)

    A. A clinic or health facility

    B. A school

    C. A seminar or training group

    D. A private home

72. The role of consultants in problem solving processes does not include serving:
    (Average Rigor) (Skill 4.1)

    A. As an advocate

    B. As an expert in a particular area

    C. As a school official

    D. As a process specialist

73. Procedures in the consultation process include all except:
    (Average Rigor) (Skill 4.1)

    A. Relationship building

    B. Monitoring of the process of behavior change by a neutral party

    C. Evaluation and summarization

    D. Diagnosis of the problem

74. The consultation process in the school setting does not include:
    (Rigorous) (Skill 4.1)

    A. Eliminating the need to counsel students

    B. The meeting of a consultant and a consultee

    C. The solving of a specific problem

    D. Involving consultees (people seeking solutions to student problems)

75. The role the counselor can take in assisting participants in the consultation process does not include:
(Easy) (Skill 4.2)

A. Demonstrating classroom behavior management techniques

B. Describing the nature of the problem

C. Teaching specific skills

D. Helping devise strategies to change behaviors

76. In the consultation process, communicating student's needs to others does not include:
(Average Rigor) (Skill 4.3)

A. Making a judgment by the counselor to others as to what is best for the student

B. Clarifying the needs of the student with the student

C. Opening lines of communication between the consultee and the student by having open dialogue

D. Balancing the needs of the student and the consultee so each can understand the other's position

77. Procedures for successful communication with parent/guardian(s) in the consultation process do not include:
(Average Rigor) (Skill 4.4)

A. Informing parents frequently as to the progress of the resolution of the problem

B. Using parents as a valuable source of information about the student

C. Accepting parents ideas for behavior modification

D. Explaining the problem in simple language as parents are probably unaware of all ramifications

78. Contributions of parents to the consultation process do not include:
(Easy) (Skill 4.4)

A. Family and medical history

B. Usually parents do not contribute to the process, as they are uncooperative

C. Monitoring the child at home

D. A positive attitude

79. **In gathering data for the implementation of a consultation, the counselor should not include:**
 (Easy) (Skill 4.5)

 A. Examine the permanent record card for test scores and patterns

 B. Gather medical and discipline history

 C. Consult with an administrator about the student's family history

 D. Talk with the student's teachers to see if they are experiencing the same type of problems

80. **In conducting a consultation follow-up the counselor should not**
 (Rigorous) (Skill 4.6)

 A. Gradually decrease participation in the process

 B. Reevaluate after a period of time

 C. Interview the consultee to determine if there is continuing progress

 D. Interview the student and parents in regards to their satisfaction with the consultation

81. **Data included in the initial referral of a child to a counselor should not include:**
 (Average Rigor) (Skill 5.1)

 A. Unverified illegal behavior

 B. Academic history

 C. Behavior and discipline history

 D. Family history

82. **Valid reasons a student may have for wishing to drop a course are all of the following except:**
 (Easy) (Skill 5.2)

 A. Too heavy an academic load

 B. Conflict between the student and teacher

 C. Lack of proper background in the subject area

 D. Falling behind due to hospitalization and frequent legal absences

83. Procedures for referring a student to an outside agency do not include:
    (Average Rigor) (Skill 5.2)

    A. The counselor has evaluated a need for long-term counseling

    B. The parent feels the child has an emotional problem and asks for an evaluation

    C. The counselor is mandated to report a sexual abuse case

    D. The student doesn't like the counselor

84. Techniques to let the community know what is happening in guidance do not include:
    (Easy) (Skill 5.3)

    A. A guidance newsletter

    B. A letter to the editor regarding the school board cutting guidance staff

    C. Speaking about the guidance program to local civic organizations

    D. Involving community leaders as members of an advisory board

85. A regular series about guidance in the local paper does not include:
    (Easy) (Skill 5.3)

    A. Monthly guidance activities

    B. Notification of test and scholarship dates

    C. Feature a student of the month

    D. Opinions about school administration policies

86. A good guidance program does not include:
    (Easy) (Skill 5.4)

    A. A pay scale for counselors higher than other staff members in order to attract quality people

    B. An adequate budget to supply the basic tools needed for the program

    C. Trained, certified, professional counselors

    D. A mission statement

87. The goals of the guidance program should not include:
(Rigorous) (Skill 5.4)

A. Acquisition of academic skills by the student population commensurate with their abilities

B. Acquisition of personal insights by students

C Learned ability to make intelligent choices

D. Selection of a lifetime career

88. Service that guidance counselors do not deliver is:
(Easy) (Skill 5.4)

A. Testing

B. Cafeteria and hall monitoring

C. Personal counseling

D. Education and career counseling

89. Components of a program of parental contact do not include:
(Average Rigor) (Skill 5.4)

A. Informing parents of information heard around the school regarding their child

B. Creating a parent advisory committee

C. Telephone contact with parents when students are doing well

D. Small teas and home meetings to inform parents of procedures for their children to maximize education opportunities

90. Components of an orientation program should include each of the following except:
(Easy) (Skill 5.5)

A. Advance notice by mail

B. Invitations to the entire community

C. A tour of the facilities

D. Introduction of counselors and administrators to students and parents with a description of their roles

91. The success of a child in school does not depend on: *(Rigorous) (Skill 5.5)*

   A. Class size

   B. Home attitude towards education

   C. Initial positive introduction to the school experience

   D. Addressing the specific needs of each child

92. Who are not the people limited to a "need to know" basis with regard to student assessment data: *(Average Rigor) (Skill 6.1)*

   A. The newspapers

   B. School personnel

   C. The counselor, psychologist, school social worker and principal

   D. Attorneys

93. Written permission must be obtained to release assessment data from: *(Average Rigor) (Skill 6.1)*

   A. The counselor

   B. The student over 18 or the student's parent or guardian

   C. The Board of Education

   D. The teacher who generated the assessment data

94. Guidelines for ethical behavior written in the ACA Code of Ethics and Standards of Practice include all of the following areas except: *(Rigorous) (Skill 6.2)*

   A. Penalties for specific ethical violations

   B. Confidentiality

   C. Resolving of ethical issues

   D. Relationships with other professionals

95. **The purpose of the National Board of Certified Counselors (NBCC) is to:**
    (Average Rigor) (Skill 6.2)

    A. Issue practice credentials

    B. Resolve ethical issues

    C. Certify professionals to assure a high level of competence

    D. Bargain for higher salaries for guidance professionals

96. **When an ethical issue arises in a counselor's practice the counselor should:**
    (Average Rigor) (Skill 6.2)

    A. Refer to the ACA code of Ethics

    B. Decide what to do immediately so the problem will not linger

    C. Ask the client what to do

    D. Consult with the Board of Education

97. **Parents, guardians, and students have a right to all the following records except:**
    (Rigorous) (Skill 6.3)

    A. Copies of all records relating to the student

    B. Copies of all student records containing comparisons of the student with other students

    C. All the student's records maintained by public institutions

    D. A list of all types of records directly related to the student

98. **The rights of parents, students, and guardians does not include:**
    (Average Rigor) (Skill 6.3)

    A. Right of access

    B. Right of privacy

    C. Right to challenge and a hearing

    D. Right to alter the written record if they feel it is not true

99. The penalty in the event public school officials refuse to comply with parent's rights does not include:
(Easy) (Skill 6.3)

A. A right to sue the offending institutions

B. The right to a hearing within a reasonable period of time

C. The right to be awarded attorney and court fees

D. The right to withdraw the student from school

100. The intent of the Individuals with Disabilities Act of 1975 was all of the following except:
(Rigorous) (Skill 6.4)

A. To give children with disabilities special services to make up for past discriminations

B. To give children with disabilities a free and appropriate education

C. To provide for the needs of children with disabilities

D. To prevent discrimination against children with disabilities

101. The Individuals with Disabilities Act does not require:
(Rigorous) (Skill 6.4)

A. A free and appropriate public education for all children with disabilities

B. The federal government to devise and implement all state FAPE programs

C. An annual IEP for each child classified as disabled

D. Equal access to educational programs that are provided to all children in the district

102. Possible signs of child abuse do not include:
(Easy) (Skill 1.7)

A. Old clothing

B. Frequent bone fractures

C. Self-destructive behavior

D. Poor hygiene

103. Indications of substance abuse do not include:
 (Easy) (Skill 1.7)

 A. Attention problems

 B. Non-participation in athletic activities

 C. Bizarre behavior

 D. Unawareness of surroundings

104. Individual learning styles can be expressed in relation to all the following except:
 (Rigorous) (Skill 7.1)

 A. Environmental factors

 B. Emotional factors

 C. Intelligence quotients

 D. Sociological elements

105. Physical elements involved in learning styles do not include:
 (Average Rigor) (Skill 7.1)

 A. Auditory

 B. Kinesthetic

 C. Visual

 D. Temperature

106. Post secondary education opportunities are not offered in:
 (Average Rigor) (Skill 7.2)

 A. Vocational training

 B. Community colleges

 C. The military

 D. Practical experience

107. Post-secondary educational opportunities do not depend on:
 (Average Rigor) (Skill 7.2)

 A. The type of career in which the individual has an interest

 B. The abilities of the individual

 C. The social status of the individual

 D. The costs involved in attending

108. Reliable sources of information on scholarships and financial aid do not include:
(Easy) (Skill 7.3)

   A. The guidance counselor

   B. Local scholarships

   C. Newspaper advertisements and paid financial aid sources

   D. Local and guidance department libraries

109. Financial aid specifically earmarked for women and minorities is least likely to be found in:
(Easy) (Skill 7.3)

   A. General financial aid references

   B. Minority and women's organizations

   C. The publication "The Higher Education Money Book for Women and Minorities"

   D. Local minority houses of worship

110. The type of research in which counselors would engage is not:
(Rigorous) (Skill 8.1)

   A. Historical

   B. Single subject experimental

   C. Assessment and evaluation

   D. Qualitative

111. The purpose of research in which a working counselor would not engage is:
(Average Rigor) (Skill 8.1)

   A. Basic research to obtain knowledge without the need for practical application

   B. Applied research to obtain general ways to improve education

   C. To develop a theory for creating generalizations

   D. Action research to immediately apply results to a specific problem

112. The research evaluation stages of the CIPP model do not include:
    (Rigorous) (Skill 8.2)

    A. Context evaluation

    B. Process evaluation

    C. Input evaluation

    D. Program evaluation

113. Formative evaluation does not involve:
    (Rigorous) (Skill 8.2)

    A. Collection of data in the developmental stage of research

    B. Collection of data in the implementation stage of research

    C. Collection of data after a program has been in place a period of time

    D. Collection of data when the research is in the operational stage

114. The determining factors of the worth of a program do not include:
    (Rigorous) (Skill 8.3)

    A. The program fitting preconceived ideas of outcomes

    B. Statistical significance

    C. Interpretation of the meaning of the results

    D. The practicality of implementing the program into every day use

115. Program objectives are:
    (Average Rigor) (Skill 8.4)

    A. Created to fit the outcomes of the research

    B. Readjusted as the need arises

    C. Determined after the program has been operational for a period of time

    D. Formulated before the research is instituted

116. Children's development is affected by all of the following factors except:
    (Average Rigor) (Skill 1.2)

    A. Gender and race

    B. Religion

    C. Their caregivers' emotional availability

    D. Nutrition

117. A positive school environment:
    (Average rigor) (Skill 9.1)

    A. Is the primary responsibility of the school counselor

    B. Cannot be effectively determined without good testing instruments

    C. Is created by an attitude of collaboration and care

    D. Is difficult to achieve in today's world

118. In using students as a resource in peer leadership the counselor should:
    (Average Rigor) (Skill 9.1)

    A. Not be present when students are conducting a group

    B. Choose the leaders from potential drop-outs

    C. Try not to let parents know what the process involves

    D. Have the student leaders go through an extensive period of training by a professional

119. Positive school environments have all of the following characteristics except:
    (Easy) (Skill 9.1)

    A. Strict rules

    B. Clear adult leadership

    C. Respect for diversity

    D. Policies and procedures to ensure the safety of everyone in the school community

120. **Factors related to homelessness or migrant worker status may make it difficult for students to:** *(Rigorous) (Skill 1.7)*

    A. Get a job after high school

    B. Get to school and/or attend in class

    C. Succeed in school

    D. Make friends at school

121. **All of the following are good prevention approaches except:** *(Average Rigor) (Skill 9.1)*

    A. Informing parent/guardian(s) about their child's behavior in the school setting

    B. Programs on conflict resolution and communication skills

    C. Anger management groups

    D. Special programs such as the Lunch Bunch

122. **All but which of the following are important aspects of crisis intervention:** *(Average Rigor) (Skill 9.2)*

    A. Accurate information for those affected by the situation

    B. The latest news reports about the crisis

    C. A school crisis response plan

    D. A systematic way to inform school personnel about the actions to be taken

123. **In conducting a program needs assessment the following individuals should be included:** *(Rigorous) (Skill 8.4)*

    A. Students only

    B. Administrators only

    C. People in the community who have no students in school

    D. The community, students, staff, administrators, and parents

124. Before introducing new and innovative programs to the guidance curriculum the counselor should first: (Rigorous) (Skill 8.4)

A. Ask the administration for a budget for the program

B. Conduct a needs assessment survey

C. Arrange for a pilot program

D. Contact Board of Education members to get them to agree on the implementation of the program

125. In evaluating a newly created program, the counselor should: (Rigorous) (Skill 8.4)

A. Ask the guidance staff if they think the program is working

B. Ask students informally what they think of the program

C. Conduct an extensive evaluation of all involved that includes surveys, questionnaires, and observations

D. After three months, evaluate the program and make a recommendation

ANSWER KEY

1. C	32. D	63. A	94. A
2. B	33. A	64. C	95. C
3. D	34. C	65. C	96. A
4. A	35. D	66. B	97. B
5. D	36. B	67. D	98. D
6. C	37. D	68. A	99. D
7. A	38. A	69. D	100. A
8. B	39. B	70. B	101. B
9. B	40. D	71. D	102. A
10. D	41. C	72. C	103. B
11. C	42. A	73. B	104. C
12. A	43. D	74. A	105. D
13. D	44. B	75. A	106. D
14. B	45. C	76. A	107. C
15. C	46. A	77. D	108. C
16. A	47. B	78. B	109. A
17. C	48. D	79. C	110. B
18. D	49. B	80. A	111. C
19. A	50. B	81. A	112. D
20. B	51. D	82. B	113. C
21. C	52. C	83. D	114. A
22. B	53. A	84. B	115. D
23. D	54. B	85. D	116. B
24. B	55. B	86. A	117. C
25. A	56. C	87. D	118. D
26. C	57. D	88. B	119. A
27. A	58. A	89. A	120. B
28. C	59. D	90. B	121. A
29. D	60. B	91. A	122. B
30. A	61. C	92. C	123. D
31. C	62. A	93. B	124. B
			125. C

Rigor Table

	Easy %20	Average Rigor %40	Rigorous %40
Question #	13, 25, 26, 27, 30, 36, 37, 55, 64, 71, 75, 78, 79, 82, 84, 85, 86, 88, 90, 99, 102, 103, 108, 109, 119	1, 4, 7, 8, 9, 10, 12, 17, 18, 20, 22, 23, 31, 34, 38, 42, 45, 46, 47, 50, 56, 61, 62, 63, 68, 70, 72, 73, 76, 77, 81, 83, 89, 92, 93, 95, 96, 98, 105, 106, 107, 111, 115, 116, 117, 118, 120, 121, 122	2, 3, 5, 6, 11, 14, 15, 16, 19, 21, 24, 28, 29, 32, 33, 35, 39, 40, 41, 43, 44, 48, 49, 51, 52, 53, 57, 58, 59, 60, 65, 66, 67, 69, 74, 80, 87, 91, 94, 97, 100, 101, 104, 110, 112, 113, 114, 120, 123, 124, 125

Sample Test Answers and Rationales

Directions: Read each item and select the best response.

1. **Present behavior is a result of early childhood experiences, the unconscious, and the incomplete attainment of a stage in psychosexual development.**
   (Average Rigor) (Skill 1.1)

   A. Gestalt

   B. Existential Therapy

   C. Psychoanalytic Therapy

   D. Person-Centered Therapy

Answer: C. Psychoanalytic Therapy

Psychosexual development is a characteristic of psychoanalytic theory. In this instance, the key word leads to the foundation of the answer.

2. **A technique used in this therapy is the completion of a life-style assessment.**
   (Rigorous) (Skill 1.1)

   A. Existential Therapy

   B. Alderian Therapy

   C. Behavior Therapy

   D. Reality Therapy

Answer: B. Alderian Therapy

The basis of the theory is focused on the lifestyle practices of the individual. The lifestyle assessment is a key component in the information-finding process during the first session of therapy.

3. **The thinking through of irrational thoughts that have resulted in emotional problems is the basis of this theory:**
   (Rigorous) (Skill 1.1)

   A. Reality Therapy

   B. Gestalt Therapy

   C. Behavior Therapy

   D. Rational Emotive Behavior Therapy

Answer: D. Rational Emotive Behavior Therapy

The key phrase here is "thinking through irrational thoughts." Reality therapy, Gestalt therapy, and behavior therapy involve therapeutic practices that analyze rational versus irrational thoughts. The correction of these irrational thoughts and the identification of the reality of the moment is the basis of rational-emotive therapy.

4. **Dreams are analyzed by having the client describe their feelings as they act out all parts of the dream**
   (Average Rigor) (Skill 1.1)

   A. Gestalt Therapy

   B. Psychoanalytic Therapy

   C. Behavior Therapy

   D. Person-Centered Therapy

Answer: A. Gestalt Therapy

One might consider psychoanalytic therapy to be the right answer as it does involve dream analysis. However, in that theory it is the therapist who interprets the dreams based on the client's free association process to parts and symbols of the dream.

5. **In psychoanalytic therapy the technique not used is:**
   (Rigorous) (Skill 1.1)

   A. Dream Analysis

   B. Interpretation

   C. Free Association

   D. The ABC approach

Answer: D. The ABC approach

The first three answers are all techniques involved in the process of looking for meaning in psychoanalytic therapy. The ABC approach is a major component of rational-emotive therapy. This model argues that problems do no originate from events but from the beliefs based on certain events.

6. **Unconscious processes that shield the individual from threatening and anxiety producing thoughts are all of the following except:**
   (Rigorous) (Skill 1.1)

   A. Rationalizations

   B. Resistance

   C. Ego-Defense Mechanisms

   D. Sublimation

Answer: C. Ego-Defense Mechanism

Rationalization, resistance and sublimation *are* ego-defense mechanisms that the client uses in order to minimize feelings of threat and anxiety. Ego development occurs as the client becomes more aware of the unconscious and is more able to base behavior upon reality rather than fears and anxieties.

7. The process of an active organism exhibiting controlled behavior is called:
   (Average Rigor) (Skill 1.1)

   A. Operant Conditioning

   B. Modeling

   C. Counterconditioning

   D. Transference

Answer: A. Operant Conditioning

Counter-conditioning is the process of redoing the behaviors that have caused the problem and performing new behaviors that can eliminate the problem. Transference is a process where the client projects feelings concerning past interactions onto the therapist within the counseling relationship. Modeling involves observing behavior of those we wish to imitate and then performing the behaviors we have observed.

8. Questions of freedom, choice and responsibility are addressed in:
   (Average Rigor) (Skill 1.1)

   A. Reality Theory

   B. Existential Theory

   C. Behavior Theory

   D. Person-Centered Theory

Answer: B. Existential Theory

Existential theory differs from the psychodynamic and behavior theories in that it does not rely upon a deterministic view of human nature such as being controlled by irrational actions, past occurrences, and the unconscious.

9. The ability to be true to our ideas of a meaningful life and accept responsibility for the choices we make is called:
   (Average Rigor) (Skill 1.1)

   A. Phenomenology

   B. Authenticity

   C. Restricted Existence

   D. Denial

Answer: B. Authenticity

This is a direct definition of authenticity as it relates to existential therapy. While phenomenology is discussed in existential therapy, it is the method used in many existing theories to utilize subjective experiences. Restricted existence and denial may be part of the existential therapeutic work but they do not lead to the definition stated in the question.

10. The therapist, in person-centered therapy, should have all the following personality characteristics except:
    (Average Rigor) (Skill 1.1)

    A. Genuineness

    B. Unconditional Positive Regard

    C. Empathic Understanding

    D. Polarized Thinking

Answer: D. Polarized Thinking

The goal of the person-centered therapist is to focus on the client, to make him or her the expert of feelings and events experienced. For a therapist in this or any therapy orientation to have polarized thinking would be detrimental to the process. It would also for bias on the behalf of the therapist and unavailability.

11. The layers of neurosis in Perl's Gestalt theory are all the following except:
   (Rigorous) (Skill 1.1)

   A. Phobic Layer

   B. Impasse Layer

   C. Meaninglessness layer

   D. Explosive Layer

Answer: C. Meaningless layer

Each layer within Gestalt has a specific meaning or connotation. It would not make sense to have a layer that does not have meaning.

12. Turning back to ourselves things we would like to do or have done to others is called:
   (Average Rigor) (Skill 1.1)

   A. Retroflection

   B. Introjection

   C. Deflection

   D. Confluence

Answer: A. Retroflection

The three other words have meanings that are different and specific. Confluence is the blurring of awareness of the difference between oneself and the environment. Deflection is the process of distraction or inattention, making it difficult to sustain contact. Introjection is the acceptance of others' beliefs and standards without analyzing, assimilating and internalizing them.

13. The psychological needs in reality theory are all of the following except: (Easy) (Skill 1.1)

   A. Fun

   B. Power

   C. Belonging

   D. Success

Answer: D. Success

Keep in mind that the basis of the theory is to help the client attain a "success identity."

14. The WDEP model in reality theory includes all the following except: (Rigorous) (Skill 1.1)

   A. Wants

   B. Direction

   C. Evaluation

   D. Planning and Commitment

Answer: B. Direction

The WDEP model is about defining behaviors to target for intervention, setting related goals and executing practices to facilitate behavior change. *Doing*, not direction, is the step in the model when the therapist explores what clients are doing and what direction they taking in their behavior to obtain those wants and needs.

15. In cognitive behavior therapy the multimodal therapy was originated by:
    (Rigorous) (Skill 1.1)

    A. Albert Ellis

    B. Carl Rogers

    C. Arnold Lazarus

    D. Margaret Mahler

Answer: C. Arnold Lazarus

Albert Ellis founded rational-emotive therapy, Carl Rogers developed person-centered therapy, and Margaret Mahler developed object- relations theory.

16. The stages of life in Erik Erikson's psychosocial theory include all of the following except:
    (Rigorous) (Skill 1.1)

    A. Innocence vs. Generativity

    B. Basic Trust vs. Basic Mistrust

    C. Identity vs. Role Confusion

    D. Ego Integrity vs. Despair

Answer: A. Innocence vs. Generativity

Innocence is not one of Erikson's stages. Generativity vs. Stagnation is the stage when maturity is achieved. The task here is to establish and guide the next generation and come to terms with one's dreams and accomplishments.

17. **Stages of human development as outlined by Jean Piaget include all of the following except:**
    (Average Rigor) (Skill 1.2)

    A. Sensorimotor Stage

    B. Concrete Operational Stage

    C. Cultural and Environmental Stage

    D. Formal Operational Stage

Answer: C. Cultural and Environment Stage

While cultural and environmental factors may play a role throughout one's development, it is not a stage as defined by Piaget.

18. **With regard to counseling, it is beyond the scope of the school counselor's role to:**
    (Average Rigor) (Skill 1.4)

    A. Provide individual and group counseling

    B. Provide crisis intervention

    C. Provide family consultation

    D. Provide mental health evaluations

Answer: D. Provide mental health evaluations

Although school counselors may identify the need for a mental health evaluation, it is beyond the scope of their role and often their knowledge base to actually perform mental health evaluations. Referral to a community agency or private practitioner is most appropriate to meet students' evaluation needs.

19. Categories of theories of learning are all the following except:
    (Rigorous) (Skill 1.2)

    A. Behavioristic

    B. Functionalistic

    C. Associationistic

    D. Cognitive

Answer: A. Behavioristic

Theories of counseling, personality and learning are interrelated and address behavior. The three categories of learning theories are functionalistic, associationistic and cognitive.

20. In applying counseling theories to specific situations it is important that the counselor does all of the following except:
    (Average Rigor) (Skill 1.3)

    A. Create a rapport with the student

    B. Pick a theory to apply and stick to that theory.

    C. Involve the student in the decision making process

    D. Encourage the student to make his/her own decisions.

Answer: B. Pick a theory to apply and stick to that theory

It would be detrimental to the counseling process for a counselor to have such a narrow-minded focus. While the therapist can ascribe to a certain theory, the process needs to be about the client and his/ her needs. It is not uncommon for therapists to utilize multiple theories in order to meet the specific needs of the individual.

21. A disadvantage of group counseling is:
    (Rigorous) (Skill 1.4)

    A. The presence of a built in support system

    B. A non-threatening atmosphere

    C. The ability to substitute the group for the real world permitting the client unlimited time to make adjustments

    D. The counselor can reach more clients

Answer: C. The ability to substitute the group for the real world permitting the client unlimited time to make adjustments

The key words to focus on are "substitute" and "unlimited." The group experience is a one that provides individuals within the group to disclose and challenge problems as well as practice new skills. Due a variety of possible constraints, it should never be assumed that the opportunity of counseling is unlimited. Group counseling creates an alternative environment which clients sometimes begin to associate with to the exclusion of other aspects of their lives, further distorting views of reality.

22. Limitations of group counseling are all of the following except:
    (Average Rigor) (Skill 1.4)

    A. There is pressure to accept group values without analyzing them

    B. The counselor has to deal with a diverse population

    C. People sometimes function poorly in groups

    D. Individuals in the group can justify their present status by reinforcement from the group

Answer: B. The counselor has to deal with a diverse population

This answer is vague and is makes an assumption that is too general.

23. **Definitions of group dynamics include all the following except:**
    (Average Rigor) (Skill 1.5)

    A. A political ideology built on the concept of the organization and management of groups.

    B. A collection of specific techniques and concepts that describe and facilitate group interactions

    C. A branch of knowledge concerned with groups and their interactions, and interactions with other groups and individuals

    D. A way of describing the individual behavior of people

Answer: D. A way of describing the individual behavior of people

Focusing on individual behavior misses out on the dynamics of the group experience.

24. **Group dynamics is all the following except:**
    (Rigorous) (Skill 1.5)

    A. An emphasis on empirical research and theory

    B. A branch of knowledge concerned mainly with the way groups form

    C. The relationships of groups with observable phenomena

    D. The interrelationship of all social science disciplines

Answer: B. A branch of knowledge concerned mainly with the way groups form

This answer seems like it would be appropriate. However, group dynamics is about behavior within the group setting instead of looking at how groups form. Group dynamics must be considered separate from organizational structure. Both impact the functioning of the group, but dynamics will determine client needs and counselor facilitation.

25. Elements of good listening skills include all the following except:
    (Easy) (Skill 1.6)

    A. Involving strong emotions in the process of listening

    B. Being genuinely interested in the speaker

    C. Remembering what has been said

    D. Permitting a speaker to express him/herself fully

Answer: A. Involving strong emotions in the process of listening

The listener is not fully available if his/her emotions are getting in the way; this is called "counter transference." At this point the counselor is projecting their issues into the client's experience, rather than truly listening.

26. Barriers to good listening are all of the following except:
    (Easy) (Skill 1.6)

    A. Impatience with the speaker

    B. Faking Attention

    C. Being a sounding board

    D. Forming an opinion about the value of what is to be said before it is said

Answer: C. Being a sounding board

Answers a, b and d are all barriers to good listening.

TEACHER CERTIFICATION STUDY GUIDE

27. Good responding skills include all the following except:
    (Easy) (Skill 1.6)

    A. Ability to show your feelings without inhibitions

    B. Reflecting the person's feelings

    C. Giving constructive feedback

    D. Maintaining eye contact

Answer: A. Ability to show your feelings without inhibitions

Responding should be about the client, not the counselor.

28. The developmental concept not included in existential therapy is:
    (Rigorous) (Skill 1.2)

    A. Capacity for self-awareness

    B. Acceptance of responsibility for freedom

    C. Ability to direct one's life without therapeutic help

    D. Acceptance of the significance of death to the living

Answer: C. Ability to direct one's life without being introspective

The basic goals of existentialist therapy are to help clients become aware that they are free and to expand this self-awareness, to increase their choice of options on the basis of the freedom to choose other options, to accept responsibility for those choices, to recognize the factors that hinder freedom to choose, and to experience an authentic existence. Without introspection, achieving success through these developmental processes would be impossible.

29. A developmental concept not used in counseling theory is:
    (Rigorous) (Skill 1.2)

    A. Changing behavior based on present situations

    B. Freud's division of development into five stages

    C. The correction of irrational and illogical thinking

    D. Learning ways to rationalize our behavior

Answer: D. Learning ways to rationalize our behavior

Counseling theory does not teach people how to rationalize behavior or develop other ego-defense mechanisms.

30. Effective study skills do not include:
    (Easy) (Skill 1.8)

    A. Learning the material and then putting it aside until there is an exam scheduled

    B. Studying every day at a certain time

    C. Taking good notes

    D. Reviewing frequently

Answer: A. Learning the material and then putting it aside until there is an exam scheduled

The student will not retain the information if there is a large gap between the learning and the testing of the material.

31. All of the following are signs of anorexia nervosa except:
    (Average Rigor) (Skill 1.7)

    A. Malnutrition

    B. Behavior regression

    C. No outward signs

    D. Recognizable weight loss

Answer: C. No outward signs

This answer is self-explanatory. There are significant outward signs displayed when a person is struggling with anorexia.

32. Violence prevention programs do not include:
    (Rigorous) (Skill 1.7)

    A. Conflict resolution seminars

    B. Behavior modification programs

    C. Training faculty and staff to intervene before violent confrontations occur

    D. Instituting a boxing program to train students to protect themselves

Answer: D. Instituting a boxing program to train students to protect themselves

Students can be taught to respect the rights of others by programs of cooperation and conflict resolution. The violence prevention program should not promote, encourage, or prepare students to engage in physical retaliation. A boxing program is outside the scope of violence prevention.

33. Effects of stereotyping and prejudice on victims do not include:
    (Rigorous) (Skill 1.7)

    A. Confrontation of the perpetrator by the victim

    B. The development of a sense of inferiority

    C. The development of a persecution complex

    D. Harboring of thoughts of violence toward the perpetrator

Answer: A. Confrontation of the perpetrator by the victim

To confront a perpetrator could lead to a potentially dangerous altercation between to the victim and the perpetrator, although in some structured situations and with sufficient planning this can be a healing event for victim and/or perpetrator. However, such an interaction is not an *effect* of stereotyping and prejudice.

34. In helping students to make decisions, steps in the process do not include:
    (Average Rigor) (Skill 1.8)

    E. Defining the problem

    F. Listing the manageable options

    G. Surveying family, friends, and peers

    H. Formulating goals in relation to outcomes

Answer: C. Surveying family, friends, and peers

Surveying denotes a process of information gathering from friends and family; it is not a step in the decision making process.

TEACHER CERTIFICATION STUDY GUIDE

35. **Topics for discussion in the initial interview with a student to gain rapport do not include:**
    (Rigorous) (Skill 1.9)

    A. Academic progress

    B. Activities in which the student is participating

    C. Difficulties in school adjustment for the entering student

    D. Matters of discipline referral

Answer: D. Matters of discipline referral

The counseling role is not about reprimanding students. Such judgment could be detrimental to building rapport. The initial referral process is sometimes difficult for the counselor if his/her previous interactions with a student have been in consultation with the administration regarding disciplinary issues. It is of paramount importance for the counselor to not include that history or these matters in the initial interview, unless the topic is broached by the student.

36. **Ways not to be effective in communicating information to students are:**
    (Easy) (Skill 1.9)

    A. Through individual interviews

    B. Through contacting friends and parents

    C. Through home room visitations

    D. Through monthly newsletters home

Answer: B. Through contacting friends and parents

Counselor caseloads are often quite large. It is not an effective use of time for counselors to call parents just to inform them of guidance events and deadlines.

GUIDANCE AND COUNSELING

37. Some current sources of professional information for counselors do not include:
   (Easy) (Skill 1.10)

   A. Professional journals

   B. Workshops and conventions

   C. Visitations to other school programs

   D. Teenage magazines

Answer: D. Teenage magazines

Counselors should not rely on popular media as sources of professional information and best practices.

38. Advantages of holding a college night include all the following except:
   (Average Rigor) (Skill 1.10)

   A. For counselors to be able to meet with their colleagues about colleges

   B. To bring a variety of post-secondary institutions together for the benefit of students and parents

   C. To initiate students into the college/post secondary admissions scene

   D. For counselors to get to know college admissions personnel

Answer: A. For counselors to be able to meet with their colleagues about colleges

The purpose of the college night is process of fact finding and discovery for both students and counselors; its intent is for counselors to commiserate with colleagues.

39. **The inaccuracy of test results caused by chance is called:**
    (Rigorous) (Skill 2.1)

    A. Standardization

    B. Standard Error of Measurement

    C. Standard Score

    D. Derived Score

Answer: B. Standard Error of Measurement

Every test has some element of inaccuracy or unreliability due to chance so this element of the test is taken into consideration when evaluating test results and an allowance is made for this phenomenon. The degree of error is reported in the standard deviation, a specific band of scores. The formula for obtaining the standard error of measurement takes the square root of 1 minus the reliability coefficient.

40. **A statistical concept that measures the relationship between two factors in test validity is:**
    (Rigorous) (Skill 2.1)

    A. Reliability Coefficient

    B. Standard Deviation

    C. Raw Score

    D. Correlation Coefficient

Answer: D. Correlation Coefficient

The reliability coefficient is a statistical concept that measures how reliable the relationship is between two factors in test validity. The standard deviation is the interval of score differences that indicates levels of achievement. The raw score is the basic score usually obtained by counting the number of answers right. It can also be obtained by using the number of wrong answers. The authors of the test can determine any other way to define a raw score.

41. A condition that does not affect testing results is:
 (Rigorous) (Skill 2.2)

   A. The physical and mental condition of the testee

   B. The testing room environment

   C. The colors of the clothes the proctors are wearing

   D. The validity of the test

Answer: C. The colors of the clothes the proctors are wearing

There is no empirical research to date concerning the impact of the colors of the clothes the proctor is wearing on testing results. In addition to the physical and mental condition of the testee, the testing room environment and the preparation of the testee are conditions that can impact testing results as defined by research.

42. All the following are advantages of testing except:
 (Average Rigor) (Skill 2.3)

   A. As a way to get multiple test interpretations

   B. As a way to help students recognize and use the resources they have

   C. As a way to present meaningful information to the student for decision making

   D. As a way to help identify options for the future

Answer: A. As a away to get multiple test interpretations

One of the benefits of testing is to use a standardized process to provide information about the student's performance, access to success and to make recommendations.

43. **Disadvantages of testing are all the following except:**
    (Rigorous) (Skill2.3)

    A. The possibility of results being used improperly

    B. The possibility of the student misinterpreting the test results

    C. The inherent subjectivity of tests administered for counseling purposes

    D. Using the test to predict future behavior

Answer: D. Using the test to predict future behavior

One of the purposes of testing is to provide a picture of where the student is currently and to anticipate what the student needs to in order to succeed in the future. The process may include identifying barriers to learning, tools needed to increase access to learning and potentially highlighting a process that would be beneficial to the student. However, tests cannot predict future behavior with any certainty.

44. In the administration of tests, procedures should include all the following except:
(Rigorous) (Skill 2.4)

　　A. Safeguarding the tests

　　B. Informing the students of the nature of the test by giving them questions from the test

　　C. Guarding the tests in the exam room when students have access to the room

　　D. Guarding the tests by not leaving them where students and non-authorized personnel have access

Answer: B. Informing the students of the nature of the test by giving them questions from the test

Since one of the goals of counseling is to build realistic self-concepts, counselors must provide ways to offer useful feedback. Testing can be one of the tools to help students recognize their resources, utilize their strengths and accept their limitations. If students are provided with the test ahead of time, a true picture of the student's abilities and self-concept is not being identified. There is a distinct difference between counseling and instruction; the counselor's job is not to "teach the test" but to inform students of the objectives and testing parameters prior to the event.

TEACHER CERTIFICATION STUDY GUIDE

45. **In interpreting test results the counselor should not:**
    (Average Rigor) (Skill 2.5)

    A. Relate the results to the goals that had previously been determined

    B. Provide for individual interpretation

    C. Wait to interpret the tests when the student is scheduling the following year's courses

    D. Give the student input into the interpretation of the test results

Answer: C. Wait to interpret the tests when the student is scheduling the following year's courses

The work of a school counselor is to help the student maximize their performance. If a counselor delays in providing information to a student, it could contribute to student failure instead of success.

46. **If tests need to be interpreted in a group the counselor should not:**
    (Average Rigor) (Skill 2.5)

    A. Announce individual test scores

    B. Explain the norm group to which the students have been compared

    C. Provide for private individual interpretation for students

    D. Explain statistics of the test so students can understand the meaning of their scores

Answer: A. Announce individual test scores

The answers listed in b, c, and d support appropriate components of sharing information in a group setting. Providing information about an individual to a group is not only detrimental to the student-counselor relationship, but it is also unethical.

GUIDANCE AND COUNSELING

47. The written report of test results and interpretation should not:
    (Average Rigor) (Skill 2.5)

    A. Be written in understandable language

    B. Always include charts and graphs

    C. Be disseminated on a need to know basis

    D. Be written in the language of testing

Answer: B. Always include charts and graphs

Visual representations within a written report concerning test results are not necessary for understanding them; thus, it is not a critical component of the report.

48. In accurately reporting test results for interpretation by others all the following guidelines should be used except:
    (Rigorous) (Skill 2.6)

    A. A uniform method of recording should be employed

    B. Consistency in language used should be employed

    C. The purpose, limitations, and the validity of the test should be stated

    D. The receiver of the results should be required to contact the counselor in order to receive the counselor's candid opinion

Answer: D. The receiver of the results should be required to contact the counselor in order to receive the counselor's candid opinion

While it is not in appropriate to contact the counselor for further explanation or clarification of test results, seeking a "candid opinion" can misconstrue or confound the nature of the results.

49. **In interpreting test results to other professionals and parents the counselor does not always have to:**
    (Average Rigor) (Skill 2.7)

    A. Be thoroughly familiar with the test

    B. Let other staff members see the results of the test

    C. Notify the student that the counselor will be sharing the results with their parent/guardian(s)

    D. Work with the parents in a counseling relationship to help them understand their child's abilities

Answer: B. Let other staff members see the results of the test

Sharing test results with other staff should first be discussed with the student and the student's parents. Depending on the nature of the test, other personnel often do not need to know the results and it best to keep it confidential. The confidential nature of the counseling role demands caution in the dissemination of information concerning students.

50. **In interpreting testing data from other professionals and testing firms, the counselor should do all the following except:**
    (Average Rigor) (Skill 2.8)

    A. Understand the material in the report

    B. Go right to the summary and not worry about the technical aspects of the report

    C. Contact the writer of the report for clarification if needed

    D. Refer to the testing manual for clarification if needed

Answer: B. Go right to the summary and not worry about the technical aspects of the report

It is important that the counselor provide an explanation that honors the purpose and motivation for the testing. Looking at the technical aspects of the report may offer important information to this end.

51. The occupational environments of Holland's theory do not include: (Rigorous) (Skill 3.1)

    A. Artistic and social

    B. Realistic and conventional

    C. Enterprising and investigative

    D. Hostile and negative

Answer: D. Hostile and negative

While some occupational settings may in fact be hostile and negative, these adjectives do not describe the occupational environments as defined by Holland.

52. The classifications of career counseling theories do not include: (Rigorous) (Skill 3.1)

    A. Trait factor theory

    B. Developmental or self-concept theory

    C. No choice theory

    D. Personality and career choice theory

Answer: C. No choice theory

All career counseling theories are based upon the concept that people make choices, whether those choices are conscious or not. The why and how people make the choices they make varies from theory to theory.

53. **Super's theory of vocations is based upon all of the following except:**
    (Rigorous) (Skill 3.1)

    A. The inheritance of psychic energies

    B. The development of self-concepts

    C. External conditions that dictate the expression of self-concepts vocationally

    D. Developmental behavior theory

Answer: A. The inheritance of psychic energies

Psychic energy is defined as the drive that propels a person's behavior and psychological functioning. This is not part of Super's theory.

54. **Similarities in theories of vocational choice are all of the following except:**
    (Average Rigor) (Skill 3.1)

    A. They describe the relationship between two sets of observations

    B. They consider family influence on vocational choice a primary consideration

    C. They are usually based upon personality theory

    D. They emphasize the same types of critical periods in career development

Answer: B. They consider family influence on vocational choice a primary consideration

The primary influences on vocational choice include personality and level of education. Vocational choice theories place very little emphasis on the influence of family as a major factor. Family influence can have a direct impact on educational achievement but only an indirect, minor impact on vocational choice.

55. **Shadowing is not:**
    (Easy) (Skill 3.2)

    A. Spending an extended period of time with a particular person in a chosen field

    B. A paid experience

    C. A learning experience by the student and the business volunteer

    D. Experiencing the daily routine of a particular business

Answer: B. A paid experience

A paid experience or internship is provided with the understanding that services are being provided on behalf on an employee. The true shadowing experience should be experiential and have nothing to do with payment.

56. **The purpose of a career day includes all of the following except:**
    (Average Rigor) (Skill 3.2)

    A. Make contacts in the community for future job placement for students

    B. Make students aware of the qualifications needed for particular jobs

    C. Give the students a break in the academic routine while giving them a valuable education experience

    D. Make available to students, in one place, occupational information for all levels of interests and abilities

Answer: C. Give the students a break in the academic routine while giving them a valuable education experience

The purpose of career day is to provide students the opportunity to make connections between what they are learning within the classroom and marketable skills desired in the workforce.

57. Computer generated career information systems do not include:
    (Rigorous) (Skill 3.2)

    A. Choices

    B. GIS

    C. SIGI

    D. IDEA

Answer: D. IDEA

IDEA is a federal law that was passed making local and state education entities responsible for providing children with disabilities a "free and appropriate public education."

58. Decision making occurs at all the following critical points in career development except:
    (Rigorous) (Skill 3.3)

    A. When a student enters high school

    B. In selecting an entry level job

    C. When selecting education plans

    D. In changing jobs

Answer: A. When a student enters high school

According to Roe and Ginzberg, Ginzberg, Axelrad & Herm, the high school years mark a period of exploration in a person's career development. This process of exploration can provide insight to a possible career choice.

59. In the *anticipation* phase of decision making as outlined by Tiedman and O'Hara, the stages include all but:
(Rigorous) (Skill 3.3)

    A. Exploration

    B. Crystallization

    C. Clarification

    D. Reevaluation

Answer: D. Reevaluation

The four stages of the anticipation phase are exploration, crystallization, choice, and clarification.

60. In Tiedman and O'Hara's *accommodation* phase of decision making the stages include all but:
(Rigorous) (Skill 3.3)

    A. Induction

    B. Initiation

    C. Reformation

    D. Integration

Answer: B. Initiation

The three stages of the accommodation phase include induction, reformation, and integration.

61. **In evaluating education and career materials all the following should be considered except:**
    (Average Rigor) (Skill 3.4)

    A. Appropriate vocabulary for the targeted age and reading level

    B. Verified accuracy of the information

    C. Material from advertisements and trade organizations

    D. The avoidance of the use of biased and stereotyping images

Answer: C. Material from advertisements and trade organizations

Counselors must use their research and investigative skills to discern appropriate education and career materials.

62. **In evaluating content of career information all the following areas should be included except:**
    (Average Rigor) (Skill 3.4)

    A. The impressions of the reader as indicated by filling out an evaluation form

    B. The preparation required for entry level jobs

    C. The work setting and conditions of the career

    D. The long-term employment outlook

Answer: A. The impressions of the reader as indicated by filling out an evaluation form

The phrase "impressions of the reader" denotes one of subjectivity instead of specific points that can provide the most comprehensive picture of a respective career. Guidelines for the preparation and evaluation of career and occupational literature have been compiled by the National Career Development Association (NCDA).

63. Methods of identifying materials to be used for career development include all of the following except:
    (Average Rigor) (Skill 3.5)

    A. Read all material on the market and eliminate inappropriate material

    B. Acquire good reference knowledge

    C. Monitor new information as it enters the system

    D. Have an organized system of reviewing material

Answer: A. Read all materials on the market and eliminate inappropriate material

In addition to the options provided in b, c and d, counselors can use the Occupational Literature Reviewer's Rating Form provided by the NCDA.

64. Levels of career development can be divided into the following time periods
    (Easy) (Skill 3.6)

    A. At the high school level

    B. At the college and young adult level

    C. At the time of marriage and children

    D. For older adults and those nearing retirement

Answer: C. At the time of marriage and children

Periods of career development are divided primarily by age and school level. Major periods of skill development include the primary school years through high school, college and beginning career, and continuing education as an older adult. Job availability, status, and salaries further characterize these periods.

65. The major steps in Zunker's 1994 model for using assessment results in developmental career counseling are:
    (Rigorous) (Skill 3.6)

    A. Analyzing needs

    B. Establishing the purpose of the test

    C. Administering a complete battery of tests

    D. Utilizing the results of assessment

Answer: C. Administering a complete battery of tests

Zunker, with influence from other theorists, established a model for the use of assessment results in developmental career counseling. There are four major steps: analyzing needs, establishing the purpose of testing, determining the instruments to be used, and utilizing the results in decision making for training and education. Identifying specific tests are more useful than using a whole battery of tests.

66. Some methods of teaching students to develop employability skills are:
    (Rigorous) (Skill 3.7)

    A. Participation in a supervised job experience

    B. Write an essay about ways to get a job

    C. Award course credit for participation in a program of job preparation

    D. Have students interview potential employers to determine what they look for in employees

Answer: B. Write an essay about ways to get a job

Having the students write essays about ways to get a job does not guarantee that they will gain employability skills. There needs to be a practical application of skills to facilitate development. Writing and communication are highly employable skills, but do not fall under the responsibility of the counselor as part of career counseling.

67. The role of the counselor in assisting students in exploring career and educational options includes all the following except:
(Rigorous) (Skill 3.7)

   A. Have material for exploration easily accessible

   B. Support and encourage students in their search for career choices

   C. Help students form realistic decisions

   D. Explain career choice theories to them

Answer: D. To explain career choice theories to them

The counselor can use one or more career theories or orientations in order to provide a framework for the work they do with students. However, merely explaining theories to students is neither an effective use of the counselor's time nor does it provide practical applications by which the students can use to explore careers and related information.

68. Sources of information on education and vocational choices include:
(Average Rigor) (Skill 3.5)

   A. Neighbors and relatives

   B. American Trade School Directory

   C. The career guide of private schools *Getting Skilled, Getting Ahead*

   D. The local library

Answer: A. Neighbors and relatives

While neighbors and relatives can provide information about their experiences with careers or jobs they have held, the information gathered would be subjective and may not be relevant or accurate.

69. In evaluating the results of consultation all the following factors should be considered except:
    (Rigorous) (Skill 4.1)

    A. The feelings of the student's parents as to the success of the process

    B. The report of the consultee as to the problem solving results

    C. An attitude change in the student

    D. Empirical results of an evaluation tool

Answer: D. Empirical results of an evaluation tool

This would serve no effective purpose on the process of consultation. Assessment and monitoring of the evaluation tool is an important step in the process of improving the counseling program, but consideration of the tool should not be considered as a part of each consultation.

70. Consultation process models include all the following except:
    (Average Rigor) (Skill 4.1)

    A. Doctor/patient model

    B. Friend of the family model

    C. Behavior consultation model

    D. Mental health consultation model

Answer: B. Friend of the family model

There is not an established consultation model based on "friend of the family" and bears no effective application in the process of consultation.

TEACHER CERTIFICATION STUDY GUIDE

71. The settings in which consultation takes place can be all the following except:
    (Easy) (Skill 4.1)

    A. A clinic or health facility

    B. A school

    C. A seminar or training group

    D. A private home

Answer: D. A private home

Consultation is best done in a neutral environment.

72. The role of consultants in problem solving processes does not include serving:
    (Average Rigor) (Skill 4.1)

    A. As an advocate

    B. As an expert in a particular area

    C. As a school official

    D. As a process specialist

Answer: C. As a school official

While a school official may be part of the consultation process, they may not be trained to provide a problem-solving process. This would involve a potential conflict of interest.

TEACHER CERTIFICATION STUDY GUIDE

73. **Procedures in the consultation process include all except:**
    (Average Rigor) (Skill 4.1)

    A. Relationship building

    B. Monitoring of the process of behavior change by a neutral party

    C. Evaluation and summarization

    D. Diagnosis of the problem

Answer: B. Monitoring of the process of behavior change by a neutral party

Consultation is an active, dynamic process. Monitoring is not part of the consultation model.

74. **The consultation process in the school setting does not include:**
    (Rigorous) (Skill 4.1)

    A. Eliminating the need to counsel students

    B. Involving a consultant and a consultee

    C. The solving of a specific problem

    D. Involving consultees (people seeking solutions to student problems)

Answer: A. Eliminating the need to counsel students

Both consultation and counseling serve a vital role in the services the counselor provides. If anything, consultation can further facilitate the need to work with students through the process of counseling.

75. The role the counselor can take in assisting participants in the consultation process does not include:
(Easy) (Skill 4.2)

    A. Demonstration of classroom behavior management techniques

    B. Describing the nature of the problem

    C. Teaching specific skills

    D. Helping devise strategies to change behaviors

Answer: A. Demonstration of classroom behavior management techniques

The role of the counselor is to observe and provide constructive feedback or to provide direct support in identified areas of need. Classroom behavior management is the educator's responsibility and areas of weakness should be addressed by the school administration. The counselor in this situation is present to offer insight to support individual students from a behavioral and social aspect, not to support the classroom educator and his/her class management.

76. **In the consultation process communicating student's needs to others does not include:**
    (Average Rigor) (Skill 4.3)

    A. Making a judgment by the counselor to others as to what is best for the student

    B. Clarifying the needs of the student with the student

    C. Opening lines of communication between the consultee and the student by having open dialogue

    D. Balancing the needs of the student and the consultee so each can understand the other's position

Answer: A. Making a judgment by the counselor to others as to what is best for the student

Instead of passing judgment, the counselor's role is assist stakeholders in the student's success. The counselor's job is to educate them about the needs of the student based on information gathered from parents and teachers, review the student's academic history, and work with all parties to develop a plan of action.

TEACHER CERTIFICATION STUDY GUIDE

77. **Procedures for successful communication with parent/guardian(s) in the consultation process do not include:**
    (Average Rigor) (Skill 4.4)

    A. Informing parents frequently as to the progress of the resolution of the problem

    B. Using parents as a valuable source of information about the student

    C. Accepting parent's ideas for behavior modification

    D. Explaining the problem in simple language as parents are probably unaware of all ramifications

Answer: D. Explaining the problem in simple language as parents are probably unaware of all ramifications

It is appropriate for the counselor to take into the parent's primary language and understanding of certain procedure. This can be established by fact finding and consulting with the student before contacting the parent/guardian(s). However, it is inappropriate to make assumptions about parents' abilities and the level of understanding they bring to any process.

78. **Contributions of parents to the consultation process do not include:**
    (Easy) (Skill 4.4)

    A. Family and medical history

    B. Usually parents do not contribute to the process, as they are uncooperative

    C. Monitoring the child at home

    D. A positive attitude

Answer: B. Usually parents do not contribute to the process as they are uncooperative

Regardless of the nature of the information parents provide, inviting the parent to be one of the experts can lead to greater levels of understanding the student's background, strengths, challenges and growth areas. At times, parents' information and suggestions can help create the best possible action plan.

79. **In gathering data for the implementation of a consultation the counselor should not include:**
    (Easy) (Skill 4.5)

    A. Examine the permanent record card for test scores and patterns

    B. Gather medical and discipline history

    C. Consult with an administrator about the student's family history

    D. Talk with the student's teachers to see if they are experiencing the same type of problems

Answer: C. Consult with an administrator about the student's family history

The focus of the consultation is to gain information concerning areas of school functioning that have a direct impact on the student. The student's family history may have an impact and be important, but this information would be learned through meeting with the student and possible the family.

80. **In conducting a consultation follow-up the counselor should not**
    (Rigorous) (Skill 4.6)

    A. Gradually decrease participation in the process

    B. Reevaluate after a period of time

    C. Interview the consultee to determine if there is continuing progress

    D. Interview the student and parents in regards to their satisfaction with the consultation

Answer: A. Gradually decrease participation in the process

Follow-up should be ongoing on behalf of the counselor to reevaluate goals and the treatment plan and make adjustments where and when appropriate.

81. Data included in the initial referral of a child to a counselor should not include:
   (Average Rigor) (Skill 5.1)

   A. Unverified illegal behavior

   B. Academic history

   C. Behavior and discipline history

   D. Family history

Answer: A. Unverified illegal behavior

This information has no place in an initial referral to a counselor. If through the process of working with the student there are behaviors of concern (especially when the student is in danger to self or someone else), the counselor should communicate them to the appropriate individuals such as parent/guardian(s), social services and possibly a school administrator.

82. Valid reasons a student may have for wishing to drop a course are all of the following except:
   (Easy) (Skill 5.2)

   A. Too heavy an academic load

   B. Conflict between the student and teacher

   C. Lack of proper background in the subject area

   D. Falling behind due to hospitalization and frequent legal absences

Answer: B. Conflict between the student and teacher

Conflict between a student and teacher can have a significant impact on the student's ability to be successful in the classroom. It is critical for the counselor to consult with both teacher and student to better understand what is creating and maintaining the conflict. Once a factor or factors have been identified, the counselor can engage in developing a plan of action along with the student, teacher, and, potentially, others such as parent/guardian(s) and administrators depending on the severity of the situation.

TEACHER CERTIFICATION STUDY GUIDE

83. **Procedures for referring a student to an outside agency do not include this information:**
    (Average Rigor) (Skill 5.2)

    A. The counselor has evaluated a need for long-term counseling

    B. The parent feels the child has an emotional problem and asks for an evaluation

    C. The counselor is mandated to report a sexual abuse case

    D. The student doesn't like the counselor

Answer: D. The student doesn't like the counselor

This situation may provide an important learning or growth opportunity for both the student and the counselor if handled in an appropriate, timely and ethical manner. It is not a reason for referral.

84. **Techniques to let the community know what is happening in guidance do not include:**
    (Easy) (Skill 5.3)

    A. A guidance newsletter

    B. A letter to the editor regarding the school board cutting guidance staff

    C. Speaking about the guidance program to local civic organizations

    D. Involving community leaders as members of an advisory board

Answer: B. A letter to the editor regarding the school board cutting guidance staff

Such a letter would not be an effective way to let the community know about the guidance department, nor would it be a collaborative or positive action to take.

GUIDANCE AND COUNSELING

85. A regular series about guidance in the local paper does not include:
(Easy) (Skill 5.3)

   A. Monthly guidance activities

   B. Notification of test and scholarship dates

   C. Feature a student of the month

   D. Opinions about school administration policies

Answer: D. Opinions about school administration policies

It would be most inappropriate for a counselor to publish opinions about school administration policies. The counselor's role as described in research and the American School Counselor's Association (ASCA) guidelines does not support counselors taking such steps. Administration policies are for school administrators and members of the Board of Education to grapple with and define. As member of the school community, however, the counselor can consult with other professions about concerns and advocate for an appropriate platform to express those concerns.

86. A good guidance program does not include:
(Easy) (Skill 5.4)

   A. A pay scale for counselors higher than other staff members in order to attract quality people

   B. An adequate budget to supply the basic tools needed for the program

   C. Trained, certified, professional counselors

   D. A mission statement

Answer: A. A pay scale for counselors higher than other staff members in order to attract quality people

Professionally and ethically speaking, pay scale should not be a factor in the quality of a guidance program.

87. **The goals of the guidance program should not include:**
    (Rigorous) (Skill 5.4)

    A. Acquisition of academic skills by the student population commiserate with their abilities

    B. Acquisition of personal insights by students

    C Learned ability to make intelligent choices

    D. Selection of a lifetime career

Answer: D. Selection of a lifetime career

Counselors can and should provide events, materials and discussions about the role of career and occupation with students, teachers, parents, administrators and members of the surrounding community. A goal of the counseling program should be to facilitate career exploration. In the process of such structured and carefully planned and executed career guidance a student may feel motivated to pursue a certain career, but it is not a criterion of an effective guidance program.

88. **Service that guidance staff does not deliver is:**
    (Easy) (Skill 5.4)

    A. Testing

    B. Cafeteria and hall monitoring

    C. Personal counseling

    D. Education and career counseling

Answer: B. Cafeteria and hall monitoring

Much discussion has been had concerning the effective use of the counselor's time. Experts in the field and with ASCA do not advocate that counselors be utilized to cafeteria duty and hall monitoring. However, the reality is that some counselors are required by school administrators to provide this service.

89. Components of a program of parental contact do not include:
(Average Rigor) (Skill 5.4)

   A. Informing parents of information heard around the school regarding their child

   B. Creating a parent advisory committee

   C. Telephone contact with parents when students are doing well

   D. Small teas and home meetings to inform parents of procedures for their children to maximize education opportunities

Answer: A. Informing parents of information heard around the school regarding their child

The information that counselors share must be founded on well-researched facts. Counselors are charged as both guardians and providers of information. It would unethical to relay such information to a parent or any constituent.

90. Components of an orientation program should include each of the following except:
(Easy) (Skill 5.5)

   A. Advance notice by mail

   B. Invitations to the entire community

   C. A tour of the facilities

   D. Introduction of counselors and administrators to students and parents with a description of their roles

Answer: B. Invitations to the entire community

Part of advocating for the guidance program and its services is to utilize a variety of methods to both inform and invite.

91. **The success of a child in school does not depend on:**
    (Rigorous) (Skill 5.5)

    A. Class size

    B. Home attitude towards education

    C. Initial positive introduction to the school experience

    D. Addressing the specific needs of each child

Answer: A. Class size

County or district guidelines may make stipulations on how many students may be in a classroom. However, the success of a student can involve many but class size is not one of these factors. This is a common educational misconception.

92. **Who are not the people limited to a "need to know" basis with regard to student assessment data:**
    (Average Rigor) (Skill 6.1)

    A. The newspapers

    B. School personnel

    C. The counselor, psychologist, school social worker and principal

    D. Attorneys

Answer: C. The counselor, psychologist, school social worker and principal

The counselor, school psychologist, school social worker and the principal use student data to identity existing patterns, strengths, growth areas and action-oriented solutions to help maximize student performance and achievement.

93. **Written permission must be obtained to release assessment data from:** *(Average Rigor) (Skill 6.1)*

   A. The counselor

   B. The student over 18 or the student's parent or guardian

   C. The Board of Education

   D. The teacher who generated the assessment data

Answer: B. The student over 18 or the student's parent or guardian

Since counseling is a confidential relationship, the counselor should obtain permission from the student to release any information given in confidence. However, if the student is under 18, even if the information is gathered in reference to services provided due to a disability (i.e. IDEA qualifications), written permission needs to be procured from the parent or legal guardian.

94. **Guidelines for ethical behavior written in the ACA Code of Ethics and Standards of Practice include all of the following areas except:** *(Rigorous) (Skill 6.2)*

   A. Penalties for specific ethical violations

   B. Confidentiality

   C. Resolving of ethical issues

   D. Relationships with other professionals

Answer: A. Penalties for specific ethical violations

The key word to focus on is "guidelines." There are too many factors involved to have potential penalties discussed in the body of this work.

95. **The purpose of the National Board of Certified Counselors (NBCC) is to:**
    (Average Rigor) (Skill 6.2)

    A. Issue practice credentials

    B. Resolve ethical issues

    C. Certify professionals to assure a high level of competence

    D. Bargain for higher salaries for guidance professionals

Answer: C. Certify professionals to assure a high level of competence

It is not possible to guarantee the level of competence of counselors.

96. **When an ethical issue arises in a counselor's practice the counselor should:**
    (Average Rigor) (Skill 6.2)

    A. Refer to the ACA code of Ethics

    B. Decide what to do immediately so the problem will not linger

    C. Ask the client what to do

    D. Consult with the Board of Education

Answer: A. Refer to the ACA Code of Ethics

Rash decisions does not lend to the counselor being fluent in effective decision-making skills. The client should never be placed in a situation where he or she is expected to respond to what ethical decisions the counselor should make. The Board of Education is not an appropriate place to explore the ethical concerns of counselors.

97. Parents, guardians, and students have a right to all the following records except:
(Rigorous) (Skill 6.3)

    A. Copies of all records relating to the student

    B. Copies of all student records containing comparisons of the student with other students

    C. All the student's records maintained by public institutions

    D. A list of all types of records directly related to the student

Answer: B. Copies of all student records containing comparisons of the student with other students

Parents and eligible students only have access to their specific child's records. It would be a violation of another student's rights to have his/her information viewed by an undesignated person. Confidentiality and parent/student rights are a paramount concern for the school counselor. His/her success and the quality of the program depend on such confidentiality.

98. The rights of parents, students, and guardians does not include:
(Average Rigor) (Skill 6.3)

    A. Right of access

    B. Right of privacy

    C. Right to challenge and a hearing

    D. Right to alter the written record if they feel it is not true

Answer: D. Right to alter the written record if they feel it is not true

Parents may advocate for personal information to be corrected when they have the appropriate documentation to support the change. However, parents may not request the student's academic record be altered in any way.

99. **The penalty in the event public school officials refuse to comply with parent's rights does not include:**
    (Easy) (Skill 6.3)

    A. A right to sue the offending institutions

    B. The right to a hearing within a reasonable period of time

    C. The right to be awarded attorney and court fees

    D. The right to withdraw the student from school

Answer: D. The right to withdraw the student from school

In the event that a school or school official violates a parent's rights, the parent is entitled to seek recourse. Such recourse may include litigation seeking damages or services. Withdrawing a student from school is not a penalty guaranteed to the parent, although the parent may exercise the option of moving the child to another school.

100. **The intent of the Individuals with Disabilities Act of 1975 was all of the following except:**
    (Rigorous) (Skill 6.4)

    A. To give children with disabilities special services to make up for past discriminations

    B. To give children with disabilities a free and appropriate education

    C. To provide for the needs of children with disabilities

    D. To prevent discrimination against children with disabilities

Answer: A. To give children with disabilities special services to make up for past discriminations

IDEA is about providing students equal access to education. No one student should have more access to education services due to past issues of discrimination.

101. The Individuals with Disabilities Act does not require:
     (Rigorous) (Skill 6.4)

     A. A free and appropriate public education for all children with disabilities

     B. The federal government to devise and implement all state FAPE programs

     C. An annual IEP for each child classified as disabled

     D. Equal access to educational programs that are provided to all children in the district

Answer: B. The federal government to devise and implement all state FAPE programs

It is not the federal government's responsibility to devise or implement state programs. Also, counselors need to be aware that there is no guarantee an IEP will be issued because a student has a disability. Often, parents need to request that an IEP be written and implemented..

102. Possible signs of child abuse do not include:
     (Easy) (Skill 1.7)

     A. Old clothing

     B. Frequent bone fractures

     C. Self-destructive behavior

     D. Poor hygiene

Answer: A. Old clothing

It would be making assumption about the state of the clothing and the family situation. If there is a concern about a student's welfare, the counselor can follow up using appropriate channels and methods.

103. Indications of substance abuse do not include:
(Easy) (Skill 1.7)

A. Attention problems

B. Non-participation in athletic activities

C. Bizarre behavior

D. Unawareness of surroundings

Answer: B. Non-participation in athletic activities

Students with substance abuse issues may elect or continue to participate in athletic opportunities. However, if there is a pattern of inconsistent attendance or exhibits of behavior that is not customary for the student (providing that there is not a known medical or physical condition), follow-up is indicated.

104. Individual learning styles can be expressed in relation to all the following except:
(Rigorous) (Skill 7.1)

A. Environmental factors

B. Emotional factors

C. Intelligence quotients

D. Sociological elements

Answer: C. Intelligence quotients

Individual learning styles include environmental, emotional, sociological and physical elements. Learning styles do not measure and are not based on intelligence.

105. **Physical elements involved in learning styles do not include:**
    (Average Rigor) (Skill 7.1)

    A. Auditory

    B. Kinesthetic

    C. Visual

    D. Temperature

Answer: D. Temperature

The senses of seeing, hearing, smelling, feeling, and touching are instrumental in the way many individuals learn. Temperature is not included as one of the physical elements in relation to learning styles. It does play a role and have a substantial impact on student achievement, but is not directly related to a learning style.

106. **Post secondary education opportunities are not offered in:**
    (Average Rigor) (Skill 7.2)

    A. Vocational training

    B. Community colleges

    C. The military

    D. Practical experience

Answer: D. Practical experience

Post-secondary education lends itself to organized learning experiences, which at the end of a certain time interval, a degree is awarded to signify the completion or mastery of certain skills. While much can be learned from a practical experience such as internships or shadowing, an individual does not earn a degree or certificate. Options A, B, and C are opportunities that afford an individual to learn a skill set, be awarded a degree, and then apply for professional work experiences.

TEACHER CERTIFICATION STUDY GUIDE

107. **Post-secondary educational opportunities do not depend on:**
     (Average Rigor) (Skill 7.2)

   A. The type of career in which the individual has an interest

   B. The abilities of the individual

   C. The social status of the individual

   D. The costs involved in attending

Answer: C. The social status of the individual.

Social status will only be a determining factor if an individual allows it to be.

108. **Reliable sources of information on scholarships and financial aid do not include:**
     (Easy) (Skill 7.3)

   A. The guidance counselor

   B. Local scholarships

   C. Newspaper advertisements and paid financial aid sources

   D. Local and guidance department libraries

Answer: C. Newspaper advertisements and paid financial aid sources

Counselors, parents and students need to be cautious about advertisements for scholarships and financial aid. It is important that such opportunities be thoroughly investigated. If money is being asked for up front in order to apply for a scholarship, applicants should not apply. It is likely that such an opportunity is a moneymaking scam. There are a variety of sources that can be used to determine if a source is legitimate.

109. Financial aid specifically earmarked for women and minorities is least likely to be found in:
(Easy) (Skill 7.3)

    A. General financial aid references

    B. Minority and women's organizations

    C. The publication "The Higher Education Money Book for Women and Minorities"

    D. Local minority houses of worship

Answer: A. General financial aid references

Options B, C, and D address the sources that are specific students seeking scholarships for minorities and women. It is important when seeking scholarships with specific criteria to research sources that provide that information.

110. The type of research in which counselors would not engage is:
(Rigorous) (Skill 8.1)

    A. Historical

    B. Single subject experimental

    C. Assessment and evaluation

    D. Qualitative

Answer: B. Single subject experimental

Single Subject Experimental Research focuses on the individual and not on the results of group experimentation. It is used to test hypotheses of the effect of a particular treatment on one or more behaviors or phenomena. This type of research would not help a counselor gain the tools necessary to be able to be effective in his or her work with students.

TEACHER CERTIFICATION STUDY GUIDE

111. **The purpose of research in which a working counselor would not engage is:**
    (Average Rigor) (Skill 8.1)

    A. Basic research to obtain knowledge without the need for practical application

    B. Applied research to obtain general ways to improve education

    C. To develop a theory for creating generalizations

    D. Action research to immediately apply results to a specific problem

Answer: C. To develop a theory for creating generalizations

This answer is self-explanatory. It would be little to no use for a school counselor to formulate a theory for the purpose of creating generalizations.

112. **The research evaluation stages of the CIPP model do not include:**
    (Rigorous) (Skill 8.2)

    A. Context evaluation

    B. Process evaluation

    C. Input evaluation

    D. Program evaluation

Answer: D. Program evaluation

The CIPP (Context, Input, Process, Product) Model has four stages: Context evaluation, input evaluation, process evaluation, and product evaluation.

113. Formative evaluation does not involve:
(Rigorous) (Skill 8.2)

   A. Collection of data in the developmental stage of research

   B. Collection of data in the implementation stage of research

   C. Collection of data after a program has been in place a period of time

   D. Collection of data when the research is in the operational stage

Answer: C. Collection of data after a program has been in place a period of time

This type of evaluation involves the collection of data while a program is in the developmental, implementation, or the operational stage.

114. The determining factors of the worth of a program do not include:
(Rigorous) (Skill 8.3)

   A. How well the program fits preconceived ideas of intended outcomes

   B. Statistical significance

   C. Interpretation of the meaning of the results

   D. The practicality of implementing the program for every day use

Answer: A. How well the program fits preconceived ideas of intended outcomes

Evaluative data and the practicality of implementing a program for everyday use should guide the determination of the value of a program. Fitting into preconceived goals for outcomes is not necessarily useful in assessing a program's worth.

TEACHER CERTIFICATION STUDY GUIDE

115. Program objectives are:
(Average Rigor) (Skill 8.4)

    A. Created to fit the outcomes of the research

    B. Readjusted as the need arises

    C. Determined after the program has been operational for a period of time

    D. Formulated before the research is instituted

Answer: D. Formulated before the research is instituted

An effective guidance program needs to be based on research in order to be sound in its validity.

116. Children's development is affected by all of the following factors except:
(Average Rigor) (Skill 1.2)

    A. Gender and race

    B. Religion

    C. Their caregivers' emotional availability

    D. Nutrition

Answer: B. Religion

Development is affected by many different factors, one of which is NOT religion.

117. **A positive school environment:**
 (Average rigor) (Skill 9.1)

   A. Is the primary responsibility of the school counselor

   B. Cannot be effectively determined without good testing instruments

   C. Is created by an attitude of collaboration and care

   D. Is difficult to achieve in today's world

Answer: C. Is created by an attitude of collaboration and care

A caring approach and an actively collaborative style are major contributors to positive school environments. While schools counselors must be a part of this process, it is not their primary responsibility, nor can they effect such change alone.

118. **In using students as a resource in peer leadership the counselor should:**
 (Average Rigor) (Skill 9.1)

   A. Not be present when students are conducting a group

   B. Choose the leaders based on their popularity among peers

   C. Keep the selection and training process private

   D. Have the student leaders go through an substantive period of training by a professional

Answer: D. Have the student leaders go through an substantive period of training by a professional

Adequate training is important to the success of any peer leadership program, along with good supervision.

TEACHER CERTIFICATION STUDY GUIDE

119. Positive school environments have all of the following characteristics except:
    (Easy) (Skill 9.1)

    A. Strict rules

    B. Clear adult leadership

    C. Respect for diversity

    D. Policies and procedures to ensure the safety of everyone in the school community

Answer: A. Strict rules

While clear policies and strong leadership are essential, strict rules generally do not contribute to creating positive school environments. At times, they may even have a detrimental effect, depending on the nature of the rules.

120. Factors related to homelessness or migrant worker status may make it difficult for students to:
    (Rigorous) (Skill 1.7)

    A. Get a job after high school

    B. Get to school and/or attend in class

    C. Succeed in school

    D. Make friends at school

Answer: B. Get to school and/or attend in class

Post-traumatic stress, poverty and other life concerns may interfere with a student's attendance. She or he may not come to school or may have difficulty paying attention in class. However, students from all families can succeed in school, make friends, and get a job after high school with the right support and motivation.

121. All of the following are good prevention approaches except: *(Average Rigor) (Skill 9.1)*

   A. Informing parent/guardian(s) about their child's behavior in the school setting

   B. Programs on conflict resolution and communication skills

   C. Anger management groups

   D. Special programs such as the Lunch Bunch

Answer: A. Informing parent/guardian(s) about their child's behavior in the school setting

Telling parent/guardian(s) about what their child is doing in school may or may not be useful to either the parents or the child. It is not a prevention approach, though at times it may be part of a consultation or problem-solving effort.

122. All but which of the following are important aspects of crisis intervention: *(Average Rigor) (Skill 14.1)*

   A. Accurate information for those affected by the situation

   B. The latest news reports about the crisis

   C. A school crisis response plan

   D. A systematic way to inform school personnel about the actions to be taken

Answer: B. The latest news reports about the crisis.

Although the media may provide some useful information, for the most part, attending to news reports if not helpful in providing good crisis intervention. Crisis responders need to get information from reliable sources, such as emergency management or law enforcement personnel. Further, the sensationalistic nature of news reports can feed fear and create unnecessary anxiety.

123. In conducting a program needs assessment the following individuals should be included:
    (Rigorous) (Skill 8.4)

    A. Students only

    B. Administrators only

    C. People in the community who have no students in school

    D. The community, students, staff, administrators, and parents

Answer: D. The community, students, staff, administrators, and parents

It is imperative that all members of the school community including parents are given the opportunity to provide feedback about guidance counseling services; this is the only way in which counselors will generate a clear picture of the needs of the community. The integration of all stakeholders is key to the success of any needs assessment.

124. Before introducing new and innovative programs to the guidance curriculum the counselor should first:
    (Rigorous) (Skill 8.4)

    A. Ask the administration for a budget for the program

    B. Conduct a needs assessment survey

    C. Arrange for a pilot program

    D. Contact Board of Education members to get them to agree on the implementation of the program

Answer: B. Conduct a needs assessment survey

Just because a program is innovative and has a lot to offer does not mean it will meet the needs of the respective school community. It is critical for school counselors to have a pulse on the needs of the community they serve. It is imperative that the school counselor develops a program improvement model that clearly outlines action steps for the creation, monitoring, and support of any and all programs that are utilized.

125. In evaluating a newly created program, the counselor should:
(Rigorous) (Skill 8.4)

    A. Ask the guidance staff if they think the program is working

    B. Ask students informally what they think of the program

    C. Conduct an extensive evaluation of all involved that includes surveys, questionnaires, and observations

    D. After three months evaluate the program and make a recommendation

Answer: C. Conduct an extensive evaluation of all involved that includes surveys, questionnaires, and observations

Using formal and organized methods of assessment provides structure to the information-gathering process as well as makes it easier to compile statistical information.

XAMonline, INC. 21 Orient Ave. Melrose, MA 02

Toll Free number 800-509-4128

TO ORDER Fax 781-662-9268 OR www.XAMonline

FLORIDA TEACHER CERTIFICATION EXAMINATIONS - FTCE - 2008

PO# Store/School:

Bill to Address 1 Ship to address

City, State Zip

Credit card number _____-_____-_____-_____ expiration__

EMAIL _____

PHONE FAX

13# ISBN 2007	TITLE	Qty	Retail	Total
978-1-58197-900-8	Art Sample Test K-12		$15.00	
978-1-58197-689-2	Biology 6-12		$59.95	
978-1-58197-046-3	Chemistry 6-12		$59.95	
978-1-58197-047-0	Earth/Space Science 6-12		$59.95	
978-1-58197-578-9	Educational Media Specialist PK-12		$59.95	
978-1-58197-347-1	Elementary Education K-6		$28.95	
978-1-58197-292-4	English 6-12		$59.95	
978-1-58197-274-0	Exceptional Student Ed. K-12		$73.50	
978-1-58197-294-8	FELE Florida Ed. Leadership		$59.95	
978-1-58197-619-9	French Sample Test 6-12		$15.00	
978-1-58197-615-1	General Knowledge		$28.95	
978-1-58197-586-4	Guidance and Counseling PK-12		$59.95	
978-1-58197-045-6	Humanities K-12		$34.95	
978-1-58197-640-3	Mathematics 6-12		$32.95	
978-1-58197-597-0	Middle Grades English 5-9		$59.95	
978-1-58197-662-5	Middle Grades General Science 5-9		$59.95	
978-1-58197-286-3	Middle Grades Integrated Curriculum		$59.95	
978-1-58197-284-9	Middle Grades Math 5-9		$59.95	
978-1-58197-590-1	Middle Grades Social Science 5-9		$59.95	
978-1-58197-616-8	Physical Education K-12		$59.95	
978-1-58197-044-9	Physics 6-12		$59.95	
978-1-58197-657-1	Prekindergarten/Primary PK-3		$73.50	
978-1-58197-695-3	Professional Educator		$34.95	
978-1-58197-659-5	Reading K-12		$59.95	
978-1-58197-270-2	Social Science 6-12		$59.95	
978-1-58197-583-3	Spanish K-12		$59.95	
			SUBTOTAL	
ndling $8.25 one title, $11.00 two titles, $15.00 three or more titles				
			TOTAL	